CONTENTS

01   **CHAPTER ONE**
Why The Pandemic Merely Accelerated The Top Priority Imperative

17   **CHAPTER TWO**
How To Connect Your Impact To Their Priorities

33   **CHAPTER THREE**
Meet Your Prospect: The Three-Pound Lump

47   **CHAPTER FOUR**
Messaging Your Why

59   **CHAPTER FIVE**
Find Your Priority Position

71   **CHAPTER SIX**
Win The Brain

85   **CHAPTER SEVEN**
Win The Journey

97   **CHAPTER EIGHT**
Win The Deal

111   **CHAPTER NINE**
The New Playbook

123   **CHAPTER TEN**
Into The Future

APPENDIX

134 Acknowledgments

135 About The Author

136 Works Referenced

Praise for *The Priority Sale*

"Examining how the brain makes buying decisions allowed us to develop a brand story that actually made a difference for our members. Paired with the behavioral strategies for our staff, it's made our work more rewarding and, as a result, more profitable, too."

Cindy Duke, CEO, Natco Credit Union

"*The Priority Sale* is exactly what my team needed. Not only have we improved how we sell, we've enjoyed doing it. I believe, now, we are having more purposeful and meaningful engagements."

Mike Harmon, Chief Sales Officer, New Era Technology

"Our marketplace is crowded, and it was easy for our team to get caught up in features and benefits selling. The Priority Sale changed that. We have different—and better—conversations with our prospects today."

Raymond Canzanese, Vice President Business Development, TouchPoint, Inc.

"In a world where everything is changing so fast, the way we were selling before was not immune. The Priority Sale gave us an understanding of the real impact we have for our prospects, which in turn has enabled a consultative approach in our team that works. We know our role in the marketplace and have fewer conversations with prospects who think of us as 'just another' in our industry."

Steve Niesman, President Americas Region, NTT DATA Business Solutions Inc.

"The Priority Sale is refreshing and a breath of fresh air to the new selling environment. Bryan and his team bring a great program that refines our good habits, introduces new habits and methodologies, and provides structure that brings positive change to the sales process we are using."

Chris Manning, Commercial Director, The Shepherd Color Company

THE PRIORITY SALE

HOW TO CONNECT YOUR REAL IMPACT
TO YOUR PROSPECTS' TOP PRIORITIES

BRYAN GRAY, PAUL DAVISON,
JESSE LAFFEN, AND MIKE RENDEL

INDIE BOOKS
INTERNATIONAL®

© 2021 by Revenue Path Group

All rights reserved.

Printed in the United States of America.

No part of this publication may be reproduced or distributed in any form or by any means without the prior permission of the publisher. Requests for permission should be directed to permissions@indiebooksintl.com, or mailed to Permissions, Indie Books International, 2424 Vista Way, Suite 316, Oceanside, CA 92054

Neither the publisher nor the authors are engaged in rendering legal or other professional services through this book. If expert assistance is required, the services of appropriate professionals should be sought. The publisher and the authors shall have neither liability nor responsibility to any person or entity with respect to any loss or damage caused directly or indirectly by the information in this publication.

The views and opinions in this book are those of the authors at the time of writing this book, and do not reflect the opinions of Indie Books International or its editors.

The Priority Sale® is a registered trademark, number 88932734, of Revenue Path Group.

ISBN-13: 978-1-952233-62-3
Library of Congress Control Number: 2021909292

Designed by Mike Rendel and Joni McPherson of McPherson Graphics

INDIE BOOKS INTERNATIONAL®, INC
2424 VISTA WAY, SUITE 316
OCEANSIDE, CA 92054
www.indiebooksintl.com

1

Why The Covid-19
Pandemic Merely
Accelerated The Top
Priority Imperative

We believe the biggest current threat you face is becoming a commodity in your prospect's eyes. And what's making it worse? Decision-making teams keep getting bigger, and they are ignoring you until the very end of their buying journey.

This is driving a race to the bottom, caused by what we call the three deadly Cs: *commoditization*, *compressed* selling time, and *consensus* decision-making. This race will not stop on its own and we believe sales teams are unprepared and ill-equipped to sell the way today's buying teams expect.

Over the past twenty years, it has become harder for sales organizations to prevail over the three deadly Cs. They are a product of the rise of the internet and our roller coaster economy. This book is designed to help you combat them to win the brain, win the journey, and win the deal.

Is your company unprepared and ill-equipped for an ever-accelerating sales future? To help you decide, here is the tale of two salespeople who wanted to close a big deal, Stan and Fran.

Stan The Reactive Salesman

This is the cautionary tale of Stan, who was alerted to the opportunity of a big potential sale by his marketing team. The prospect had found Stan's company by doing an exhaustive search. What Stan didn't realize was his opportunity was just another late-stage lead.

Stan used his charm and charisma to make sure his company was on the short list. Stan's company was one of three invited to a Zoom-room showdown with an eight-member buying committee. "Wow, the buying committees keep getting larger and larger," mused Stan. Quickly, it became obvious that each member of the buying committee had his or her own agenda.

Because of the compressed selling time, Stan did not know enough about the prospect company's competing agendas. To the ears of the buying committee, Stan's pitch sounded remarkably like the other two companies', so he was a commodity.

Neither Stan nor his competitors made a case for why the prospect should even choose to take action and not just stick with the status quo. Stan's company wasted a great deal of time and energy just to tie for second place.

Fran Had A Proactive Plan

This is the tale of Fran, who was after the prize of closing the big deal. Fran understood the triple whammy: COVID-19 forced buyer behavior changes that are not going away, the rate of change is accelerating, and in this economy, only top priorities are going to get through. Fran set her sights to the C-level, two or three levels above where she usually played.

She knew face-to-face meetings are largely a thing of the past, so she asked for virtual meetings with decision-makers. When Fran landed a call with the CEO, she knew she had to capture his attention in the first minute. "Sales cycles are becoming an instant action or instant disengagement," thought Fran.

While Zoom gave her access to the CEO, Fran realized patience isn't guaranteed. She also knew she only had ninety seconds to trigger the brain of the decision-maker during the virtual meeting. She had relentlessly practiced a believable elevator pitch that followed how the brain makes decisions and connects to the threat level. Fran also knew this was a person who could set and adjust budgets if this was a top-tier priority for the company.

By connecting to the decision-maker's priority, Fran was able to make the case to move swiftly with their decision. A top priority is nothing to waste time on with a lengthy sales process. Fran won the deal by avoiding the three deadly Cs. She wasn't a commodity, she didn't get squeezed by compressed selling time, and she built consensus within the decision-making of the buying committee.

Here is the moral of the tale of Stan and Fran: In today's business, and especially during economic contractions, only the top priorities are going to get action. That means you need to outmaneuver every other solution provider to make The Priority Sale. It happens when you align your solution with the top priority of a real decision-maker in your prospect's organization.

Victory Belongs To The Priority Imperative

Time to consider the future of sales growth for your company. If you aren't prepared to move swiftly, courageously, and thoroughly, it will not be pretty.

Call it the top priority imperative. If you are not constantly seeking and solving priority problems, they won't write you a check. And no checks means bankruptcy, the ultimate form of market feedback. Instead, the feedback you want is that you are having better conversations with the right people. You are relevant to your prospects and customers.

In our work as strategic-selling change agents, we have found that in nearly every sale, sales teams do not find a real priority. They fail because they need to approach things differently and expend more effort than normal to find it. They're faced with bigger and bigger decision-making teams that have one thing on their minds:

> *Why should I choose this over the other seventeen really good ideas that are floating around the organization? Is this the real priority?*

When you can connect your offering, the real impact you can make, to the right peoples' priorities, you have a real connection. These are not the people who have to abide by a budget, these are the people who set and adjust budgets. You might need to connect to the C-suite—or beyond. Those connections lead to The Priority Sale.

To make The Priority Sale, you must overcome the three deadly Cs: commoditization, consensus decision-making, and compressed selling time. Let us ponder an all too familiar scenario.

You Are In Front Of A C-Level Exec. Now What?

You meet a C-level executive who asks you the question, "What do you do?" Gulp. Before reading on, there are three questions to consider. Have you ever wondered:

> Why is it so hard to separate
> yourself from your competitors?
>
> Why is it harder than ever
> to win over the room where it happens?
>
> Why is it so painful to lose
> opportunities you should have won?

This book will help you answer those questions. Know this: The sale really happens in the instant you connect with the prospect company's priority. That can happen in ninety seconds or nine minutes; it does not need to take nine months.

How did this pressure build up over the past few years?

Blame The Internet

To begin with, blame the internet. Many business and sales leaders remember a time when they worked without the internet. That was when a salesperson was needed to help the buyer travel their entire journey.

Think about it. Before the internet, to simply obtain information, a salesperson was needed. That meant that as soon as a prospect entered the marketplace, they were in touch. We, as salespeople, were involved early on and we knew it. We met with real decision-makers all the time. Those were the days, right?

Today that's not the case. Prospects delegate a lot of research to a lower-level employee who brings options to the table. By the time they make contact, they have decided their own solution, pigeonholed you in with some competitors, and want you to compete on price.

COVID-19 dramatically accelerated this shift. Looking at the pandemic of 2020, it was the fastest the business world has ever changed. But looking forward, it will seem slow in comparison to future acceleration. To apply an old movie line to the shift, "You ain't seen nothing yet."

The big shift has created overstaffed sales teams improperly trained to compete in today's world. Those who actively attack these changes will create outsized gains, but those who stay passive may perish. Consider yourself forewarned. Your mission is to win the brain, win the journey, and win the deal. But you don't have to lose sleep over it. There is a better way.

The Big Shift Has Created The Three Deadly Cs And Two Radically Different Playbooks

The days of relationship selling, having the buyer in your back pocket, are over. Prospects—the way they are gathering information and navigating the early sale—have now replaced the need for territorial sales reps, yesterday's information distributors.

The big shift has created today's three deadly Cs to your revenue growth:

The 3 Deadly Cs

COMMODITIZATION — COMPRESSED SELLING TIME — CONSENSUS DECISION-MAKING

1. Commoditization: To your buyer everyone looks the same, sounds the same, and acts the same. If that's a fact, then it's just a race to the bottom (lowest price wins).

2. Compressed selling time: 70 percent of your buyer's journey is complete before you're invited in. That leaves you with less time than ever to influence a decision.

3. Consensus decision-making: Decision-making teams keep getting bigger and when everyone shows up with their own agenda, you lose priority.

The three deadly Cs have created such a shift that we have two completely different playbooks: the prospect's and yours (the seller's). If your playbook is not executed, you will default to the buyer's. Every time. It is a fast track to commoditization.

You will not be able to get in early enough—you will be stuck trying to win over a buying committee with little or no connection to their organizational priorities. They will have lined up a collection of similar firms, and we begin the race to the bottom.

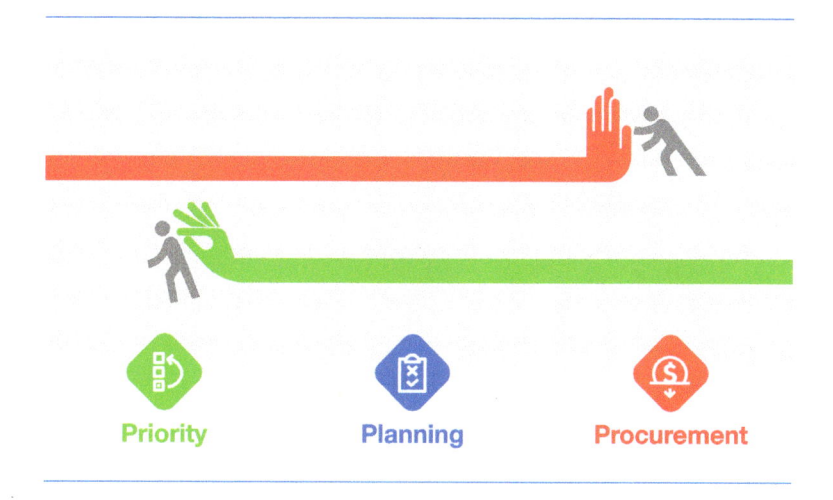

Priority — **Planning** — **Procurement**

The unprepared and ill-equipped salespeople are on track to become fulfillment specialists. Is that a job title worthy of the compensation that is usually given to salespeople? (No.)

Prospects today are probably wondering why they even must deal with a salesperson at all. Which leads to a thought-provoking question.

Why Do You Still Have Salespeople?

This may seem absurd, but if you are going to move forward, it requires some reflection. For those of us who started selling before the internet, it was an easy question to answer. Salespeople were information distributors. Think about how the prospects got their information; from trade shows, magazine articles, phone calls, and the like. We needed more people because we could not let our competitors win that space. We all went out and created a force of salespeople, traipsing across the land and working to educate prospects. We had to, to make sure we didn't miss an opportunity.

In those days, you could even have had an inferior product and sold it for a higher price. If you had superior coverage compared to your competitors, you could still win. Sounds quaint now, doesn't it?

So, back to the question: Why do you still have salespeople?

A common answer today may be along the lines of:

> *I want to make sure the prospect fully understands the reason(s) we should be considered. We have distinct value and if prospects really understood this, they would choose us based on that, not on price.*

That is a reasonable answer. But how can this occur if you are brought in at the last minute, being asked to compete on nothing but price?

When you are following the buyer's playbook, this happens again and again. By the time they contact you, the real decision-maker has likely exited the scene. The time to have reached them was months prior when you could have connected with their priority. Now, they have decided what they want. They're unlikely to pay much attention to what you have to say.

So, the question again: What is the real value of salespeople today? Consider this answer instead:

> *To hunt down decision-makers, then connect our real impact to their highest priorities before they even realize they have a problem.*

That's more like it!

Differentiators Are Not That Different

Companies search endlessly for differentiators, driving themselves crazy in the process. At best, they produce a list of features, not value. Meanwhile, the prospect is trying to figure out what the hell to do about the problem they are having and wondering why nobody seems to be able to help. Both parties miscommunicate, creating frustration on both sides.

A CEO told us the following story:

> *I was at a conference where I ran into the contact for one of our biggest accounts. We exchanged pleasantries before the conversation led to very direct talk about an upcoming contract she would be bidding out.*
>
> *Over the course of that conversation, she asked me a pointed question. It came from an honest place; she was not being malicious or mean about it. She said, "Tell me, why do we work with your company? Oh, and you can't say your people make the difference."*
>
> *I was stopped dead in my tracks. I couldn't answer the question. All I wanted to say was that our people really do make the difference. I knew we had to figure out that answer.*

If your company has ever spent time looking for or documenting differentiators, you are losing the battle and the war. Because differentiators are not acted on. Priorities are.

The companies that win are not trying to figure out how one feature of their solution can make a marginal difference. They are finding C-suite executives and solving their problems.

Today's salespeople must be able to connect their real impact to their prospect's top priorities. They must get in at a higher level, earlier. They must do it in a way that separates them from an ever-expanding list of alternatives. They must be able to reach larger decision-making team members with their own priorities, with less time than ever to take on every good idea or potential initiative.

Introducing The Priority Selling Approach

Priority selling was founded on the belief that we have moved beyond a manipulative and persuasive sales environment. Prospects will no longer be "cornered." Even if they are, they have more than enough information at their fingertips to fight back. Prospects will try to vet candidates and make decisions on their time and schedule.

Salespeople who cling to the old ways, attempting to still sell down this traditional path, will be quickly identified and tossed out. And that's okay. Let's face it, if they aren't adding any value to the equation, they don't deserve the chance to sell.

The Priority Sale requires early access, and early access requires an old sales behavior that has taken on new importance.

Hunters Gotta Hunt

Hunting—finding good prospects and meeting real decision-makers—is the responsibility of today's sales rep, not the marketing department. Real value starts here, and if you are not performing this role, you are failing your prospect.

Hunting is about becoming more valuable earlier in the buyer's journey—valuable enough to be brought into the fold. Once in, you become influential enough to avoid the race to the bottom. It cannot be just a few experienced sales reps who do this; it must be every single salesperson you have. And it must be operationalized throughout your organization. In fact, even those relationship salespeople are now experiencing a much different world. They must be just as prepared.

The leads you're getting from marketing are procurement requests. The prospect has already named a solution, their information gathering is complete, and that is why they called you or submitted that web form. While some of these may become sales, you are already playing by the buyer's playbook, by their rules, and on their timeline.

The Priority Sale begins with hunting. It finds the *real* priority behind the sale and it helps the salesperson regain their role, contributing value, rather than fulfilling orders.

The Priority Sale's three foundational principles:

1. We need an approach and teaching method built for the way prospect teams buy. Selling teams deserve a positive and welcome alternative to the buyer's

current playbook; designed to get you in earlier and become more influential with higher-level decision-makers.

2. We must use what we know about the brain, and how it makes buying decisions. A relentless focus on targeting and speaking clearly to the deciding part of the brain is the path to clarity and faster decision-making.

3. Connecting your real impact to your prospect's top priorities is the only way to make good sales today. Unlike outmoded sales training focusing on manipulative tactics of heroic salespeople, messaging is crucial to executing today's playbook. Your ability to gain a priority position depends entirely on your ability to execute the right message at the right time.

Why focus on the prospect's priorities? In today's business climate, only top priorities have a chance to become deals. No matter the condition of the economy or the product or solution you are selling, competition is fiercer than ever before.

Budgets are always said to be tight. Committee sizes grow in good times and bad alike. Doing nothing is an option for your prospects.

It is no longer a question of whether they are going to buy from you or a competitor. They are going to buy from you, or a competitor, or no one, or use the budget for the office holiday party.

Connecting with your prospect's top priority is not a given, and access to it is not easily granted—yet it remains the key component to the modern sale.

This is not something that marketing can simply solve. It requires changes in the behaviors and skills of your salespeople. It's why hunting is the leading part of the methodology. Armed with messaging, belief, and a connection to the decision-maker's priority, you will be able to execute your playbook. You will get in sooner, before your competitor, and align with their priorities. You will create internal champions. You will be able to rally believers who can foster support. In other words, you will have someone willing to fight for you.

The question is, *Are you worth fighting for?*

2

How To Connect Your Impact To Their Priorities

History will look back on the year 2020 as one of profound change. The B2B selling world suddenly accelerated and found itself five years into the future over the course of a few months. Sales teams had to adapt to new technologies and new realities that they would have slowly acclimated to later. These fundamental changes did not suddenly evaporate once everyone could safely return to work.

The sum of these new realities is this: because only top priorities will get approved and acted on, you need to quickly become your prospect's top priority. To do so, you will have to practice and reinforce an entirely new skill set, one that is aimed squarely at becoming a priority.

So, how do you connect to a priority of your prospect? It starts with an understanding of what a priority really is. A priority is a commitment to solve a threat.

To better understand that, let us look at a few things that are not priorities:

- A pain point that we have learned to live with, like using a spreadsheet instead of new software that could improve the outcome of the task

- A threat we would like to eliminate but are not acting on, like knowing that we need continuous sales training, but putting it off until next year's budget

- An aspiration—even one we are acting on—that does not represent a real threat, like a company softball team

You must uncover your prospect's true priority, then align your solution as the way to eliminate the threat it represents. To do so, we must understand the biology of how human brains make buying decisions.

Nothing new

Consider this familiar scenario: You have many good meetings with the prospect where a lot of learning happens. You prove a phenomenal return on investment, yet you do not get the deal. Why did you lose? It comes down to the fact that you could not successfully connect with the buying-decision part of their brains. In other words, you could not make yourself a priority. When you do not connect, there is no urgency. What is not urgent will not become a deal. It's as simple and as hard as that.

There are a few challenges you must overcome to make a successful priority connection. First, you must understand their true priorities. Second, you must connect your real impact to these priorities. Success in both tasks is based on trust, specifically the trust your prospect has in you, the salesperson.

Trust is required for the prospect to share their real priorities in the first place. It is also required for the prospect to accept that your solution is the right one. Your first task, then, is to establish that trust as quickly as possible. That is a tall order because you start at a baseline of zero.

> **Priority Sale Adage**
> Attention is fleeting; priorities are persistent.

Neuroscience discoveries show how priorities are established at the primitive brain level. In this part of the brain, the only thing that matters is keeping you alive. This is where reactions to immediate threats happen. Think about a ball that's thrown at your head. The instant decision to duck or block or catch the ball is made instinctively, by the primitive brain. This part of the brain cannot compare things. It cannot count. It does not rely on logic or facts; those things are too slow to stop the ball. It relies on instinct and reacts immediately.

Everything we encounter is first processed by the primitive brain, even buying decisions. This means that decision-making is largely emotional, not logical. So how can you persuade the emotional (primitive) part of the brain?

Most decisions are connected to a pain or threat (either physical or social) that a person desperately wants to go away. We often have aspirations but rarely act on them. We're able to live with pains that are not eliminated. However, pains that become threats get our immediate attention every time.

This is not to say that, as a salesperson, you should manufacture threats for your prospect. Truth is, you couldn't if you tried. Quite the opposite—you can only connect to priority through an existing threat in your prospect's mind.

Threats are big motivators. There is nothing stronger than the drive and desire to make these threats quickly go away; that is what makes a threat a priority. We have found most organizations struggle because they have been unable to connect their real impact to a prospect's existing threat, their existing priority.

It may seem simple, but it's not. As humans, we usually cannot articulate the threats we face. That's because threats are processed in our primitive brain which cannot process complex thoughts or form language. Yet, it is always scanning to find threats and then find a resolution to them. Scanning happens as quickly as the brain reacts to any physical threat, more often than we blink or breathe.

The primitive brain is hardwired to react fast when it comes to threats. Speed matters. If you wonder why you have ever been told to get to the point, it is because you are of no use to your prospect's brain. Threats are priorities, and if you are not a priority, there is no time for you.

At the end of the day, everything else is just background noise. It might be logical and interesting to the rational brain, but the rational brain is not listening, at least not at first. To even get the attention of the rational brain, you must give the primitive brain a reason to let you in. It's a gatekeeper to the rational brain. The way past this gatekeeper is acknowledging a threat you can help them eliminate.

Priorities are worth fighting for. So, the question is, *Are you worth fighting for?*

Are You Worth Fighting For?

If you want to be worth fighting for, you have to connect to an existing threat, and you have to do so with a higher-level decision-maker. Connecting too low on the organizational chart might be easier, but those employees rarely go to bat for you. If they do, few of the higher-ups listen.

You must gain access to a high-level decision-maker and activate your solution based on an existing threat they are facing.

Unfortunately, many salespeople do not feel they are worthy of a higher-level conversation. This is reinforced again and again because they are denied access. When this happens, it is easy to assume these prospects consider salespeople to be unworthy of higher access. This is not true.

The real reason is that too many salespeople are trying to get the appointment based on *what* they do. High-level executives do not buy *what*. That is for others to do. They buy *why* you will solve a problem—a threat—for them. Consider the following opening to a sales call:

> *We're one of the nation's leading integrators for this software platform. Can I talk to whoever is in charge of buying it?*

Who is in charge of buying it? Some low-level employee that fulfills orders for upper management, that's who. To get higher access, you must connect with why. Consider the following instead:

We've found that there are three reasons why you can't ever get what you want out of your software platform. Let's spend fifteen minutes so I can show you how other companies are overcoming them.

Connecting with *what* you sell leads to low-level conversations, with the wrong people, too late in the buyer's journey. Connecting with *why* you should be brought in makes all the difference. More on this later.

Who Is Fighting For You?

The level and degree of influence of those fighting for you really matters. Have you ever been successful connecting to a lower-level buyer's priority and then could not get the sale made? What do you think happened?

The obvious answer is that these folks were not capable of single-handedly awarding you the work. They tried but they got overruled, right? It doesn't quite work like that.

Most real decision-makers are not monarchs. Their sole opinion does not become the Law of the Land just because they say so. They listen to their team, and they also attempt to steer them in a preferred direction. Likewise, lower-level members of the buying committee take direction from decision-makers. Sure, they will voice their opinions, but eventually they fall in line. Even if they really believe in you, they risk too much by sticking their neck out for you.

Often, when a salesperson is unsuccessful, they believe that their main contact got voted down, but that is not usually the case. They did not get overruled; you just had the wrong person fighting for you. They were not the champion that can rally, then carry, the rest of the committee.

And currently, most salespeople are selling way too low in an organization. They are not equipped to get to the real decision-makers. There are several reasons why:

- They do not have valuable insights, a way to teach a C-suite member something about her current reality that reframes a threat and provides clarity.

- They do not have anything else to say that could grab a CEO's attention—just some marketing pieces they use as a crutch.

- They are responsible for pipeline moves and meetings, so they take the first appointment they can get, just to move the (wrong) needle.

Once connected at the top level, you can more easily connect to organizational priorities. And organizational priorities find their way to be connected to individual decision-makers, who are the buyers you want to reach early on. To reach the right people, we need a tool that's gone by the wayside but needs to be brought back. It's commonly known, but rarely used correctly. It is the elevator pitch.

Why You Need An Elevator Pitch

You must improve your elevator pitch game if you want to make The Priority Sale. The term *elevator pitch* was invented to describe a brief description of what you do. It's supposed to be short enough to be used in a brief elevator ride (hence the name), and comprehensive enough to fully describe what you do. Think of it as the first twenty to forty-five seconds of your sale. It should be the reason your prospect wants to listen further.

In that brief time, though, we answer the wrong question. Your prospect doesn't need to know what you do, not yet. Right now, your prospect needs to know two things:

- Why should I even listen to you right now?
- Why should I care?

Your elevator pitch must quickly answer those two questions. Even though it is called an elevator pitch, it typically does not take place in an elevator. The concept is still useful, as you only have a short amount of time to make a big impact. You will use it when you introduce yourself in most situations.

Your elevator pitch is the fastest way to connect your real impact to your prospect's priority. Of all the communication tools needed in The Priority Sale, your elevator pitch is the most crucial and must be the most powerful tool in your box. It is the leading edge in equipping your team to sell effectively. They'll use it no matter when they are brought into an opportunity or who they are talking to.

Conduct An Elevator Pitch Challenge

Elevator pitches are vitally important for The Priority Sale. The confidence that a solid elevator pitch can give your team is essential to opening doors and aligning beliefs. However, most do not understand that a lack of a powerful elevator pitch is one of the reasons why they cannot get earlier meetings with higher-level people.

So, try this: have each member of the sales team give their elevator pitch, simple as that. Give them forty-five seconds or less to see if any of them can touch on a threat that is a priority to a C-level prospect.

Elevator pitches addressing a prospect's threat get you in earlier in the process and at a higher level. They award you the next fifteen minutes of attention at the right level in an organization.

The buyer's playbook does not account for this type of connection. Their goal is to bring in the finalists after 80 percent of the buying journey has been completed. For your selling playbook, you need to counter that effect, to get in earlier in the process. You need to interrupt their buying process in order to gain access to their priority. Your elevator pitch is the leading edge to do this.

When executed well, this interruption causes the buyer's playbook to become ineffective. It opens the door for you to start helping them understand how your solution will solve a threat, matching a priority.

Effective elevator pitches are delivered in a way that builds trust because they connect the dots in prospects' brains. They make you, the seller, credible to the buyer. They foster the buyer's curiosity. An effective elevator pitch creates a mutual belief.

It is understood that long-form trust is the real making of a relationship. Yet, it is incredibly challenging when strangers meet for the salesperson to gain trust. Why is that? For starters, ask yourself: what do you think they believe your initial motive to be? If they believe your motive is to sell them something, why would they have any incentive to trust or share anything with you? If your motive, instead, is to help eliminate a mutually agreed-upon threat, then you're on to something. When others believe the same things as you, trust is quickly built.

As we'll explore in depth later, the primitive part of the brain makes unconscious decisions and acts without much thought or logic. That means you can't approach with facts and figures to make your case, at least not at first. Your prospect approaches you with an inherent fear that you're out to get their money. So, you must overcome this fear of your being that stranger wanting to take something scarce from them for something that will only benefit you. The best way to do this quickly is to show them that you share similar beliefs. This is the basis of forming trust. This connection is swiftly made or lost at the primitive level.

Elevator pitches are needed throughout the buyer's journey, especially as you meet new prospects who need to trust and believe in you. When done right, you become the mouthpiece for the decision-maker, who then uses you as a credible source to get others to better understand what they have been trying to say for too long. You become worth fighting for.

Elevator pitches:

- Build trust quickly and connect to a priority.
- Quickly tell which prospects will (and, as importantly, will not) be a good fit.
- Lay a course for conversation.

What Makes A Great Elevator Pitch?

Let's say you are successful at getting a conversation (probably virtual, these days) with a decision-maker. Whatever you do, do not begin by talking about yourself. That may seem obvious, yet so many conversations start with "a little bit about what we do." Instead, open with something powerful that will create value.

Begin your first few precious seconds with their pains and threats. Then tell a story about them. Do not start with a story because this is a contest to win over the primitive brain. If you start with a story, you will lose the brain.

From there, you are going to engage in a conversation. A brain that is conversing about how to solve its pains is a fully engaged brain.

When you have a conversation with a decision-maker, you must first break down the natural barrier that exists between you. They know they will have to say no to most of the salespeople they talk to. If they get to like you, it is just going to be harder to say no. They will feel bad. So naturally, they create a barrier.

Your job is to break down the barrier with a conversation. Speak to their threats in a way that builds trust quickly. Sharing a mutual belief in a common threat is a fast way to establish trust and find their priority.

Talking about pains alone will not get you there; they are just not painful enough. Prospects have too many pains, many of which they choose to live with. The magic lies in going a bit deeper with a pain, finding a real threat behind it. The objective is to connect at the primitive brain level. By the time you hit their threats, the connection is made.

Later, we'll talk about the necessary emotional lift to take them out of their threats, but that lift doesn't occur unless you acknowledge these threats. So, how do you find them in the first place?

How To Answer "What Do You Do?"

Author Judy Carter was on a plane and a C-level executive sitting next to her asked a question. Carter relates, "I bet it is a question you get asked all the time: 'What do you do?'" The way she answered that question made her $160,000.

"So how did I answer that question? I first started by asking her, 'Tell me a little about what you do and your business.'"

The lady talked about all the stress she deals with while working in HR and dealing with non-military contractors. "The mood and the department are just dismal, we can't keep up with demands, the government is constantly changing things on us, people are working long hours, and everybody is cranky," said the executive.

Then Carter gave her elevator pitch that addressed the threats.

"All right, let me tell you what I do," said Carter. "You know how change and all the new government policies like you are dealing with and downsizing creates all this frustration?

"Well I spent years as a headlining stand-up comic, I wrote a book that was on 'Oprah' about how to turn problems into punchlines, and I speak on stress reduction. I use a very unusual technique: I speak on the techniques of comedy, using something as simple as your sense of humor to solve problems. And believe me, I know about problems, especially from growing up with an alcoholic father. So, what I do is I show people how to use comedy and improv as a communications and stress-reduction tool. I show people how not to leave their sense of humor at home, but how to use it appropriately and even use it as a speaking and leadership tool. What are the results I get? Well my clients tell me after I speak that they hear laughter at work. Let us face it, Corporate America has become humor-impaired. People need laughter, and that laughter has great results as conflict turns into camaraderie, people communicate better—one client even said after I spoke people were saying, 'Thank God it's Monday.'"

This total stranger on the plane said to Carter, "Oh my God, do we need you!"

"She hired me fifteen minutes into the flight," said Carter. "And that turned into speaking gigs for many areas of the military: the Air Force, the Army, and spouse groups. I got so many referrals, all from that one stranger on a plane asking me 'What do you do?'"

3

Meet Your Prospect:
The Three-Pound
Lump

So why use threats to connect to priority? It's common to think that recognizing threats may lead to an adverse reaction from your prospect. It's true, and that is why it is important to do so. That adverse reaction is the only way to wake up the brain, meet it where it is, and start making real progress.

Your prospect's brain (and yours, too) is constantly scanning for threats. If you, the salesperson, show up and do not activate this part of the brain, the prospect's brain stays in idle mode, waiting for you to be done so they can move on to the next thing.

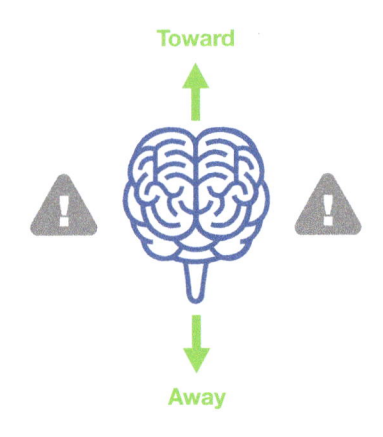

Many salespeople think they can win their prospects over by appealing to aspirations, fulfilling simple informational needs, or showing them a better version of themselves. It rarely works and just won't get the same level of attention as acknowledging a threat. Why?

It's a part of our survival mechanism. Our brains work first to keep us alive by maintaining a level of health and comfort known as stasis. Aspirations, wishes, and wants are things that get us above stasis. Pains and threats drag us below it. Our brains will react quickly to these things and our brains and bodies will work much, much harder to get back to stasis than to rise above it. To some, that is a disheartening realization. But our survival instincts are important, and they have worked well for us as a species.

So, this is the reason why you are not selling to hearts and souls, or a gut instinct. To make The Priority Sale, you must do everything in your power to persuade a three-pound lump on top of the spinal cord, that amazing organ called the brain.

While the brain is a fascinating and complex organ, it is a primitive and predictable decision-maker. When it encounters something new, a stimulus, it can only move toward it or away from it.

The brain requires outsized resources. It makes up only a small percentage of your body mass. Yet, it requires a high percentage of your blood flow and calories to keep it awake and engaged. It's the highest energy-consuming organ we have.

Ever wonder why you don't want to present an hour after lunch? That's because the stomach is consuming most of its energy at that moment. The brain is drained of resources. That also goes for the brains you are presenting to.

If you cannot wake up the brain and gain its attention, how on earth can you expect to make a sale? Not sure about you, but we've never heard anyone say, "You know, salesperson, I couldn't stay awake and I didn't listen to a word you said. But gosh, I can't wait to buy from you. Stay here, I'll get the checkbook."

So why don't humans just use the rational brain more often? Seems like we could get a lot more done and burn even more calories while we're at it. Win-win, right? The problem is, we're just not built like that.

To avoid using too many calories and too much blood flow (therefore robbing the rest of the organs of vital nutrients) our bodies wisely use what has been allocated. The logical part of the brain uses a disproportionate amount of energy. That's why you can feel tired after thinking really hard for a long period of time. But the brain actually hates to waste energy. Therefore, it continually seeks to make easy decisions without the rational part. The easier the decision, the less energy consumed.

So, to preserve energy, every decision starts in the primitive brain. Guess what? Most decisions end in the primitive brain, too. Either way, the rational brain doesn't get involved until the primitive brain decides that it is worth the energy. That is why you must start with the primitive brain and work your way up. The primitive brain is the decider or the gatekeeper.

Rational

Primitive

In fact, when it comes to decision-making, it is useful to categorize these two parts of the brain (primitive and rational) as either an influencer or decider. You might be surprised to learn that neither logic nor reason is the decider. They are influencers, offering support for big decisions, but only some of the time at that. This part of the brain follows up once the primitive brain has decided what it wants. It can reverse a decision or prevent an action, but it rarely does. It only activates once the priority has been made.

Most of the time, logic and reason just validate the decision; they rationalize whatever the primitive brain wanted to do in the first place. In short, human brains are lazy on purpose. That is part of what has kept us alive for so many generations. And when it comes to making big, important decisions—like what to buy from whom—our biology still causes us to think this way. The Priority Sale accepts this. Knowing that the brain thinks quickly, has a distinct process, and is extremely self-centered is a good thing. That's just how it protects itself.

This recognition allows you, the salesperson, to finally pitch in a way that doesn't fight it, that allows the brain to work the way it wants, and to find priority faster than ever before.

It's Not Rocket Science; It's Brain Science

The real decider is the instinctual part of the brain we call the primitive system. Its job, every second of every day, is to find and eliminate pains, especially threats. This applies to physical or social threats; it makes no difference to the primitive brain. This is ground zero for priority. Knowing that every sale relies on matching your real impact to your prospect's top priorities, you must become highly effective at reaching this part of the brain.

[Handwritten note: Also knowing how people react to threats]

The Primitive Brain: Some Things To Know

- It can only move toward a stimulus or away from it.
- It does not know how to read.

WHY?

Primitive

- It makes extremely fast decisions, but those decisions are not always right.

- Does not make inferences, and cannot connect the dots.

It is amazing that 90 percent or more of our daily choices regarding bodily functions only happen in the primitive part of the brain. They are the sort of subconscious choices the brain makes all the time, like braking when a light turns red, tying a shoelace that has come undone, or avoiding a hornet flying near you.

As well as it does in navigating things like that to keep us alive, it has some shortcomings. Since it cannot compare things, it easily becomes confused. You may think that when this happens, it would pass that confusion up to the rational brain where a comparison can make sense of things, but that is not what the primitive brain wants to do.

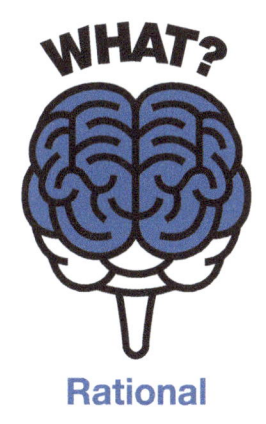

Rational

Instead, it will first attempt to ignore it altogether. The primitive brain hates to waste energy, and engaging the rational brain is going to require a lot of energy. When a decision is necessary but the primitive brain doesn't allow the rational in, it results in analysis paralysis.

When your prospect is faced with a lot of information, the kind they get from an internet search to find you, they tend to shut down.

> **For Science Geeks Only**
>
> For those who like nerdy brain science (like us), the primary structures within the primitive system include the amygdala, hippocampus, thalamus, hypothalamus, basal ganglia, and cingulate gyrus. The amygdala is the emotion center of the brain, also known as the switch, that triggers the fight or flight response. Science tells us this is the part of the brain focused on survival and keeping us alive. If you want a deeper dive into brain science, we recommend *Thinking, Fast and Slow* by Nobel Laureate Daniel Kahneman. His work was foundational to the field of behavioral economics, and this book is an easy-to-understand view into the principal concepts he developed early in his career, along with Amos Tversky.[1]

But that doesn't always happen. For the remaining small percentage of the decisions we make—those rational-brain choices—the primitive brain is still the gatekeeper. It decides when to include the rational brain and when to exclude it. If it so chooses, it will use emotion to spark action next. Logic only arrives at the end, coming in as back up support to justify what was decided.

Many parts of the brain rationalize a decision once it has been made on an emotional level. The rational brain is where all the data crunching and logical thinking happens. Many are surprised to learn that we rarely use our rational brain, because the primitive brain is so worried about survival and avoiding pain that it rarely engages with the rational.

You cannot avoid it. Every human decision, including your sale, begins with an assessment of pains and threats. After that, the brain needs a compelling story that will trigger the emotion to act.

However, it will not go there on its own because the brain is lazy. This laziness is actually a good thing, because it saves resources. It takes a lot of energy to run a brain. Your job as a salesperson is to take the brain where you want it to go. It's willing to go along for the ride. But only if you allow it to work the way it wants.

The Primitive Brain Goes To The Movies

The primitive brain is in charge, even when you go to the movies. Let us say you go see a scary movie. You watch as five clueless kids are hunted by a homicidal maniac with a chainsaw, or an unsuspecting boyfriend is captured by racist psychopaths for unwanted brain surgery. As the horror film unfolds, you scream and writhe in your seat. That is because your primitive brain is in charge and is projecting you into this story.

Now your rational brain could reason, "These are just actors. They drove their Tesla to the set and stopped off at Starbucks on the way. Really, this is just a movie and I really should relax." That is the logical decision. But logic is not in charge of your survival; the primitive brain is.

The primitive brain does not distinguish a fictional story from reality. Emotions kick in to protect you. This is the same reason you jump when you see a stick in your pathway because the primitive brain reacts as if it were a snake. The emotions of "Snake!" get triggered. As the literary character Don Quixote said of his imaginary enemies, the windmills, "They might be giants." To the primitive brain, they might be snakes.

The emotion-trigger function of the primitive brain is why you need to tell a compelling story that is prospect-focused. If the story centers on you and your firm, the prospect's self-centered brain will disengage.

Why So Many Fail To Win The Brain

Let's look at the most common ways to pitch and apply what we know about the brain to what is going on in conference rooms and teleconference lines across the world. How many times have you been in this pitch? How many times have you given this one?

> *Thanks for being here, everyone. Before we begin, we'd like to tell you a little about who we are and what we do.*

[margin note: I'm never in a "pitch" it's a longer process]

CHAPTER 3   **43**

> *We've been in business for forty-seven years and currently operate in seven locations in two countries. We have 850+ clients, including a few you may have heard of...*
>
> *Our people really make the difference, with a combined 1,250+ years of experience. We're going to go through our six core values first, and then show you our seventeen-point process for quality assurance.*
>
> *In conclusion, we think we'd be excellent partners and we hope to work with you.*

See a disturbing pattern here? Most people present in the exact opposite way that the brain processes information. By going counter to the brain's natural path, you are making a brain work harder than it wants to. Or to put it another way, harder than a brain is willing to work.

Typically, a pitch will begin methodically with an overview of the presenting firm, the logic for choosing their firm, and a discussion of the challenge. As hard as it might seem, you need to flip the presenting process upside down.

[handwritten: How will this be taught in "class"]

In this age of acceleration, teams that win understand how to focus their pitch. They will show how their product or service relieves their prospects' pains and threats. Anything more in a presentation is a distraction.

And make no mistake, brains are easily distracted. They are self-centered for a reason—keeping themselves alive. So, when you talk about yourself, your solution, and how great you are, your prospect checks out. Their brains turn to other thoughts, ones more relevant to themselves. This goes for everything you use to communicate: your website, brochures, your presentations, all of it.

Still, so many pitches lead with facts and figures, trying to win with logic, features, or benefits. But that is a big mistake. Your prospect's brain needs to hear how you are solving its pain first. Giving facts and figures up front is so different from how the brain wants its information that it's no wonder the buyer can't pay attention. You are asking their brain to do something it simply cannot.

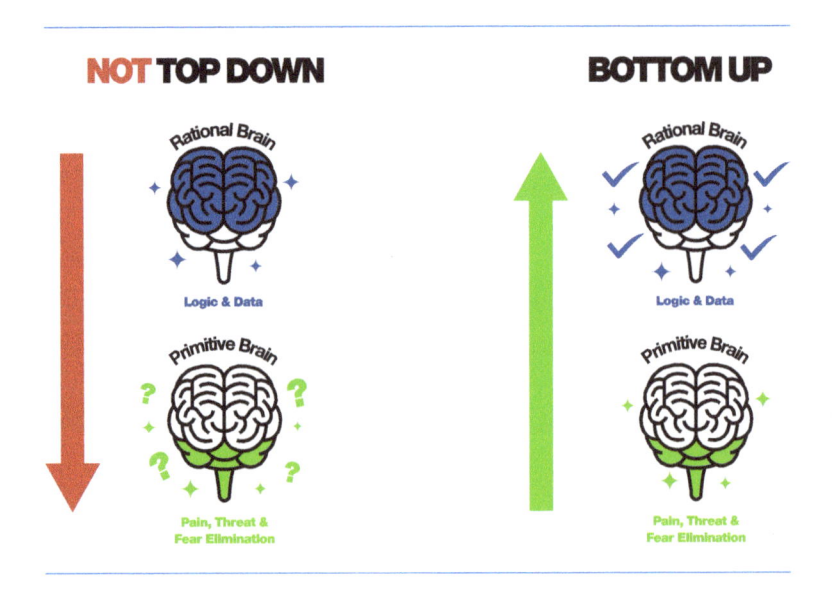

How To Use Brain Science To Sell The Team

Remember, you are not selling to one brain, you are selling to a room full of brains. Think of those ever-expanding decision-making committees as nothing more than a collection of brains that hate pain. They will only prioritize threats because threats are acted on.

Step One. Acknowledging threats they are facing is your pathway to market share gain. Start by determining what those brains want to focus on: relieving some deep-rooted, base-level threat. Use your collective brains to identify the most important threats your prospect wants to solve. Then consider how you would put it in the form of an opening question.

Step Two. Next, create the compelling reason why they should do business with you, based on the pains and threats you have raised. This should resolve the threats you have acknowledged. What is original about your firm and your approach? You might be surprised to know that it doesn't matter as much as you think. If you are executing the way the brain prefers, you do not need differentiators. You are, after all, the only solution that is going to solve the problem.

Step Three. Determine how you will prove you can eliminate these threats. What evidence can you provide that you know how to do this, repeatedly?

The Conversation You Want To Have

Let's start at the end, and work backward from your sale:

> You want to close more deals. To do so, you must connect with the united priority of an entire buying committee.
>
> For that to happen, you must connect with the priority of a high-level decision-maker that will become your

champion. Someone who will fight for you and your solution behind closed doors.

For that to happen, you must establish trust with that individual.

To establish trust, you must share a mutual belief.

To establish a mutual belief, you must recognize a common threat.

To find that threat, you start with the pains you can solve.

Next, we will use what we have learned about the brain and The Priority Sale approach to dissect selling and buying playbooks. We will find ways to make selling easier, more fun, and create happier buyers along the way.

I'm not the only one who sells

4

Messaging Your Why

The reason why your prospect should buy from you is much more powerful and important than what you do or how you do it. Yet, it is astonishing how few salespeople can articulate it. It's not their fault.

The idea of understanding and pitching the reasons why someone should buy from you is not new. In his 2015 global bestseller *Start With Why*, author Simon Sinek makes the case for starting with why.[2] Sinek popularized the concept of starting with why in his first TED Talk in 2009. The "Start With Why" video rose to become one of the most-watched on TED.com, with over forty million views and subtitled in forty-seven languages.

It is even something most sales organizations and their leaders have asked themselves and struggled with. It goes like this:

Q: Why should people buy from us?

A:
- Our widget is faster than theirs.
- We are the largest in the business.
- Our people are the best.
- We have been around the longest.
- We have better values.

So What?

If those answers sound common, it's because they are. When leadership asks their organization that simple question, they most often revert to the what or the how. They can almost never directly answer it. What is so bad about talking about what you do or how you do it?

We know that only top priorities get acted on. We also know that threats are the root of top priorities. Take another look at the list of answers. There is nothing there that instantly connects to your prospect's priority. There is no real impact.

To arrive at the actual priority, you need to think like a child. Make your list and then ask yourself "So what?" to each item. Do it repeatedly until you get to the root of the problem, the threat it represents.

Something else happens when you can address your prospect's threats. You stop sounding like everyone else. We know how easily the brain gets confused. We also know that your prospect is working from a playbook that wants you to look, sound, and act the same so you end up competing on price. Don't give in.

Those prospects wanting to commoditize you are not jerks, they're just human. They even have good intentions. They will tell you they want an apples-to-apples comparison. What they're really trying to do is make their decision easier.

But you are no apple. When you are capable of speaking to the threats they are facing, establishing mutual belief, you are different. You aren't just another option. You become the only option.

Finding Your Why

Over the years, we have developed a few tricks and shortcuts to help find your why. Here are a couple of our favorite methods.

Process Number 1: Name That Threat

The Name That Threat exercise is one that we use on a deal-by-deal basis. But if your prospects are remarkably similar from one sale to another, it may be applicable to your entire organization.

The exercise starts with naming an impact you can deliver for your customers. This might be a faster widget, reliable service, or something similar. These impacts are likely what you are using today to sell.

Then ask, "So what?" Maybe you are more reliable. So what? What does that mean for your customer?

Now, channel your inner child because we are going to get a little cranky. Ask it again. "So what?" Doing this a few times—usually three to five—can get you to a much more important place, one where you can start exploring the pains and threats your prospect is experiencing.

Process Number 2: From Flippant To Focused. "We're Not For Everybody . . ."

Have you ever heard a salesperson say this? Standing alone, it comes across as a tad arrogant, maybe even exclusive. It is too easy to say without being backed up. Yet, there is something to take away from this if you finish it. It may seem counterintuitive, but a great way to start finding your own why is to start with what you are not. To make the real connection and put substance to the statement, you'll have to frame some pain and leave a threat unresolved for just a moment.

To begin, start with the phrase "We're not for everybody."

Most sales organizations try to be all things to all people. This is one reason they struggle with understanding why prospects should buy from them. But finding and owning your why requires you to stake a claim. In doing so, you may possibly need to abandon a part of the market.

Try it on yourself. Fill in the blanks below:

"We're not for everyone. If you just want someone to _____ and not _____, then we might not be a good fit."

The first blank you fill in above should be the what you do that gets commoditized time and time again. This is usually a thing that you have had to compete on price for or have been asked to "sharpen the pencil" on. The second blank is your real impact.

For our company, Revenue Path Group (RPG), it goes like this:

> We aren't for everyone. If you just want someone to design a brochure, and not help you meet more great prospects, then we might not be a good fit.

Here are a couple more:

> For an architect:
>
> We aren't for everyone. If you just want someone to build a place for the department, and not attract more great students and faculty, then we might not be a good fit.
>
> For a parts manufacturer:
>
> We aren't for everybody. If you just want someone to crank out parts as quickly as possible, and not uncover higher margins through better design, then we might not be a good fit.

This isn't to say that you will tell this directly to your prospects, but you can. When it's executed with confidence, it is effective. Prospects will not raise their hands, say "You found me out," and then leave the room. The most common response is "That's interesting, what do you mean?" It can open doors.

There are two keys to successfully beginning a conversation this way. First, you need to have a good payoff (your "and not" statement) and to deliver it with conviction, not arrogance.

> Randy was a commercial banker for nine years before he finally figured out his bank's why. Time after time, he had collected the rate sheet from underwriting, changed the numbers on one slide in his pitch, and went into the meeting to deliver the same pitch.
>
> "Our people make the difference and we are focused on your success," he would tell his prospects. He was

not bad at it. A top performer in the company, he would make his goal some quarters.

One day he went to pitch a local retailer, with whom he had a long-standing relationship. It should have been a walk in the park but ended up being anything but.

"Sorry," his client said after reviewing the numbers. "We got another offer that knocked a few thousandths off the rate. We are going another direction. We like you guys, but business is business. I'm sure you understand."

Randy's heart sank, he could not believe it. He had gone over to their shop and locked it up one day when the client left to give birth. How could this happen? And for a few thousandths of a point on an interest rate? That only added up to a few dollars a month.

"I guess if you value a few dollars a month over long-term flexibility and security, that's a good call," he fumed. But he had stumbled on something real.

In his next pitch and forever after, he focused exclusively on the specific threats he could solve for each prospect with the flexibility and security his bank could offer.

Always Lead With Why, No Matter What

The pressure is on to engage the minds of the decision-makers. Most people get it wrong from the get-go by trying to answer the wrong questions.

In basic information gathering, the five most important questions begin with who, what, when, where, and why. This is the right formula for understanding the subject at hand.

Many well-intentioned salespeople start by answering "Who are we?" and "What do we do?" Wrong and wrong. Who and what are not the questions to lead with to create an emotional connection.

Sometimes, well-intentioned prospects or even strangers will ask "What do you do?" It may be tempting, but do not answer it.

Instead, answer the question, Why? Do it once or twice and you will soon realize how welcoming an audience you will have. The answer to why is a lot more interesting and engaging than what or how could ever be.

Best of all, leading with your why can produce the emotional connection that is imperative to build shared belief.

That is how your why builds trust fast in any situation: presentations, casual conversations, or anywhere else. With decision-making teams getting bigger and inherent delay killing your opportunities, the presenter's objective must be to help decision-makers understand why the presenter is the best and only choice.

Then, Align Your Points Of View

A powerful way to quickly establish trust is to align your points of view (POV). When your POV aligns with your prospect's, you have taken that critical first step to lowering the trust barrier.

Aligning POVs creates that immediate, deep, and visceral connection with a prospect's brain, sending a trigger that the presenter is not a threat. In fact, the right connection means the presenter is now part of their tribe. Becoming a trusted part of the tribe means beliefs are shared and relationships are strengthened.

Knowing what you believe is where your organizational passion lies, why would you want to work with companies who do not believe the same things you do?

[margin note: Have to have clear company def.]

The odds are good that when you have a mismatch of POVs, the decision-making committee is going to commoditize the presenter. This produces the feeling that the relationship is merely transactional, because it is.

The POV In Action—Elevator Pitch Part 1

Here is an example of how our company uses this point of view alignment. This is the first part of our elevator pitch. We state our POV in the form of our belief statement:

> *We believe that the biggest current threat you face is becoming a commodity in your prospect's eyes.*
>
> *What's making it worse? Decision teams keep getting bigger and they are ignoring your sales teams until the very end of their buyer's journey.*

Here is our elevator pitch at RPG. It may look familiar:

> *We believe the biggest current threat you face is becoming a commodity in your prospect's eyes. And what's making it worse? Decision-making teams keep*

getting bigger, and they are ignoring you until the very end of their buying journey.

This is driving a race to the bottom, caused by what we call the three deadly Cs: commoditization, compressed selling time, and consensus decision-making. This race will not stop on its own and we believe sales teams are unprepared and ill-equipped to sell the way today's prospects buy.

RPG is the only organization built specifically to help you battle the three deadly Cs in a way that helps you win the brain, win the journey and win the deal.

When we deliver it, it should be immediately evident who we are trying to connect with: only those who believe the same exact things. Do we believe the biggest current threat B2B business owners face is becoming a commodity? Absolutely. In fact, we believe this to the point that we also believe commoditization is the first step toward irrelevancy. So, while becoming a commodity is the biggest current threat, becoming irrelevant should be a business owner's biggest concern.

But what if you do not believe you are threatened with becoming a commodity? Prospects that do not share your belief quickly disqualify themselves. That's OK. They are not a fit. To have the confidence to quickly qualify or disqualify your organization is a skill you must perfect when executing your playbook. If you fail to do this, you will not have the positioning and confidence to sell to the (now required) higher levels in an organization. You will also waste a lot of time chasing deals that are never going to close.

Establishing The Threat—Elevator Pitch Part 2

Remember that old saying, "Don't sell features; sell benefits"? That statement does not go far enough. Today, you need to get to the payoff of the benefit right away. In other words, the benefit of the benefit. This is always the elimination of a threat.

To get there, you need to pass the So What? test. This means the benefit of the benefit must connect directly to a pain, threat, or fear. The primitive brain is always on high alert for pains and threats. Referring to these will stimulate the brain to pay attention.

How many pains should be addressed? Here the rule of three is a great guide. We know that short-term memory is fleeting, but three items are usually safe from causing confusion. Presenters should consider the three most important threats their company solves for customers like the prospect's company.

Here are the threats that our company uses in our elevator pitch:

> *This drives a race to the bottom caused by what we call the three deadly Cs: commoditization, compressed selling time, and consensus decision-making.*
>
> *This race will not stop on its own and we believe that teams are unprepared and ill-equipped to sell the way today's prospects buy.*

Providing The Emotional Lift—Elevator Pitch Part 3

Finally, it is time for the payoff to the POV alignment and the threats you have established. The payoff should be the emotional lift the prospect experiences when you have solved the threat for them with your solution.

Do not dive down into the weeds. Keep your payoff light, fast, and real. Do not overpromise but make sure it has impact. This is the final part of your elevator pitch.

Here is the emotional lift we use in our company:

> *RPG is the only organization built specifically to help you battle the three deadly Cs to win the brain, win the journey, and win the deal.*

By the way, one tip we have developed of late is that it is often useful to ask next: "What are you seeing?"

By tossing the decision-making committee a question such as that, your objective is to engage their brains with interaction. If we have successfully lowered the trust barriers and connected on the POV level, the members of the committee will offer us valuable information.

Once you can articulate your why, you can move on to deliver the Convincing Advantages of your how.

5

Find Your Priority Position

An architecture firm built a presentation over the course of several weeks for a pitch to the buying committee of a large university. The drawings were slick and the deck looked great. They had made the short list and had a good story to tell. They were an established firm with lots of experience in this type of building on these types of campuses. They were confident. The presentation went off without a hitch. It seemed like the committee was attentive and they asked questions at the end, a good sign.

Three weeks later, they got the letter. They were not selected.

"This one stings; we were clearly the right choice," one of the firm's partners said to a project manager. "This should have been ours."

The project manager replied, "You know, we live in a state where all the pitches are on public record. Maybe we should go see what was so great about the winning firm."

So, they got the transcript and sat down to look at it together.

"They led in with their history, just like us!" The project manager noticed.

"They highlighted their work on similar projects, just like us!" The principal observed.

"They also say their people make the difference, but we know ours are better," the project manager noted.

As they dissected the pitch, they realized there was not much difference at all between theirs and the winners.

"We must have come in second," they agreed.

At the end of the transcript, the committee decided—behind closed doors, but not off the record—who would be awarded the work.

"Who wants to start?" the chair asked.

One member piped up. "I like that the last firm we saw is a few miles closer to us than any of the others. That seems nice."

"Any other thoughts?" the chair asked.

Apparently, nobody spoke, because the next few lines in the transcript read like a dagger.

The chair said, "All right, all in favor?"

"Aye."

"Opposed?"

Silence.

"The decision passes, seven to zero with none abstaining. What's next?"

After reading it, the principal sat back in her chair, stunned. That is when she realized every pitch by every firm was probably the same. They probably thought they had nailed it, too. They probably told their team that if they get in the room, they will win it, too. They probably thought they came in second, too.

"If this company is ever going to reliably win business again," the principal thought, "Something big has to change."

Your Brand Is Not Gonna Save You

There has been a surge in B2B branding over the last couple of decades. It seems that B2B sales leaders and their marketing peers have looked at successful consumer campaigns for inspiration and direction. This has led to a scramble of logo updates, website work, and internal brand guardians. You know the person, who can instantly admonish you for not leaving enough space around the logo or using the wrong word for the sake of consistency.

This work has not caused any harm to these organizations, but it has been a colossal waste of time and money.

Think about Stan and Fran. It is likely that Fran's company has a nondescript name, like Dynamic Solutions, Inc. She probably uses the Inc. part of the time, or—gasp—even calls her company DSI half the time.

The thing is, none of this is getting in Fran's way. If she was involved in the sale before her prospect even understood the priority, if she helped them form the priority, her competition, Stan, doesn't stand a chance.

Sure, Stan's consistency is nice. He uses the right words and never abbreviates his company's amazing, $100,000 name. But nobody ever made a sale based on the amount of whitespace left around their logo.

Priority Position

The effort and skill to move your solution above all other potential unrelated solutions will probably be the toughest adjustment for sales teams now and into the future. You must achieve a position within your prospects' minds from which you can align to their priority. But it will not be achieved with traditional top of mind strategies, more commonly known as branding.

In fact, it may be time to rethink what a brand is, what it means, and what it can do. Today's organizations are able to quantify their return on everything. You should be able to quantify what you get from your brand.

> Your brand is your ability to position yourself in alignment with your prospects' priorities.

It's a promise to perform, first rooted in why they should use your solution now to destroy their threat.

After the why question comes the how question. Once they understand the why, decision-making committees naturally want to know how you are going to relieve their pains, threats, and fears. This still is not about you. This still is not the time to answer the "Who are we?" question.

It is tempting and very easy to dive into the details to answer "How will you do it?" Most often, people will answer with what they do. But that is not the real question the prospect is asking. In their mind, there is only one train of thought: "I am feeling pain, and it's threatening me. How do you bring relief?" It will take practice and preparation to help the prospect discover deep-rooted threats. It will take practice and preparation to master demonstrating how you will be able to relieve them.

It may seem counterintuitive, but value is not a driver of priority. Virtually every single offer from every single provider is framed as value. Lots of valuable offers go unanswered. There is a daily buy-one-get-one free deal at various pizza chains, but you aren't ordering 365 days a year, right?

Selling on value alone quickly becomes a losing game. It is not aligned with the way the prospect's brain wants to work, especially when value is articulated as a number—you are merely dancing with the rational brain. That isn't where priorities are established or where decisions are made.

In fact, those taking the value-based approach to selling are getting nowhere near what is necessary to activate the primitive brain. Do not start with value. Start with "What pains are really solved by this value?" and then quickly follow up with "What threats are then avoided?"

Answer that question for them and you have achieved a major milestone with your prospect. You have achieved what we call priority position, an actionable alignment with their primitive-brain priority. From here, every feature, every benefit, every moment of truth with your prospect must focus on their priority.

You can solve their problem. You cannot let this slip from here.

Instead of focusing on features—or even benefits—with them, you must frame them in a way that attaches to the priority. If your solution or your widget is faster than the competition, for example, show them not just how that speed will achieve their priority, really focus on its opposite. What happens when things slow down—way, way down? What are the pitfalls they will experience when they are moving slower than their competitors? <u>Keep in mind the brain will do much more to avoid a threat than to move toward a gain.</u>

Enter: Your Convincing Advantages

To answer the how question, you need to be crystal clear on how your solution relieves your prospect's pains and threats. The top three ways your company relieves those troubles is what we call your convincing advantages.

To create your Convincing Advantages, begin with the top three pains your company alleviates for customers. For each pain, create a pain-relief statement, keeping in mind that this is not about you, it is about what you do for them.

Turn your relief statements into easy-to-remember, brain-friendly messages. Your Convincing Advantages make it easy for your prospect's brain to create a quick connection, create alignment with your values, and generate action.

Here is an example from our business:

PAIN STATEMENT	RELIEF STATEMENT
Everyone sounds the same. Our prospects' messaging does not resonate with their prospects. They do not stand out from their competition.	**Win the Brain.** We help our customers attract the right prospects with brain-friendly messaging content and strategy.
They cannot seem to connect. Our prospects put barriers in front of their prospects when it comes to conversion and contact.	**Win the Journey.** We help our prospects not only connect more but connect earlier in the journey with higher-level decision-makers.
It is harder than ever to close the deal. When our prospects make it to the short list, they are daunted by commoditization, compressed selling time, and consensus decision-making.	**Win the Deal.** We help our prospects close more deals with the right set of sales tools, messaging, and confidence to answer the question, "Why should I do this now, with you?" to close the deal.

The concept is simple but not easy. Your goal is to determine the three compelling reasons you are the best and only real choice, and right now. With expanding decision teams bringing competing priorities to the table, you are now competing with more indirect competitors than direct.

Adapting will take some investment, time, and energy. It will lead to some interesting and sometimes hard conversations, but it is worth it. Think of your Convincing Advantages as the three chapters you will write for your prospects, time and time again, to show them how you are going to alleviate their pains and threats.

Your Convincing Advantages should be short, concise, and easy to recall. Alliteration (beginning words with the same sound) or rhyming are good devices that help your prospect remember them. Repetition is also helpful.

A universal truth is that the brain can easily recall combinations of three. This is often called the power of three. The brain likes options, but not too many. Three seems to be the perfect amount according to many psychologists, communication experts, and authors. Think small, medium, and large. Or beginning, middle, and end. When it comes to Olympic medals it is gold, silver, and bronze. We are easily able to compare three items at a time.

So, choose three compelling reasons why you are the best and only real choice. This may take some time, but know you can always come back to this step. Some companies create three front-runner answers, and then periodically brainstorm challenger answers to see which is superior. Above all, keep it simple and keep it focused on your prospects and their pains and threats.

Applying This To Various Stakeholders

You need to understand who you want in the room. Aligning with the wrong stakeholder often leads to aligning with the wrong organizational priority. It's less an obstacle, more of a trap that salespeople fall into.

As you now know, the number of people in the room for the average pitch continues to climb. That means you need to do your homework before the meeting. Understand, if possible, who will be there. Consider their role and their influence likely within the organization. What are their competing priorities likely to be, and how can you align your solution?

This does not mean aligning your solution to several individual priorities. You may win the moment, but the second they get behind closed doors, you've just stoked the argument. Instead, your job is to find the one priority they all share. The more you can understand their agenda, as individuals and as a collective, the better.

Convincing Advantages help unite buying committees because they offer a framework for discussing how they will compare their options. Since our brains do not want to do the heavy thinking required to construct that framework, you will be pleasantly surprised at how fast prospects will adopt yours. All you have to do is give them one. Being able to set the criteria for how they decide is, obviously, a powerful way to influence the buying decision. Yet, so few salespeople even try to.

More people in the room can be a good thing, but it can also be quite treacherous if you are not prepared. You want all the players there during the pitch because you do not want someone who was not there to lobby the decision team to delay the decision. If you cannot elevate your solution to a top priority for the entire organization, you will leave on uncertain terms. Behind the scenes, there will be infighting, with everyone defending their own priority, not yours. It leads to a typical outcome of today's B2B sale: choosing no course of action and remaining as-is.

Moving Through The Sale

Now that you understand how to form a shared priority, establish trust, craft an elevator pitch, and create your Convincing Advantages, it is time to see how to use these tools.

Each of these is based on how the brain makes (or, rather, does not make) decisions.

Next, you are going to learn how to win the brain, win the journey, and win the deal.

6

Win The Brain

To win right now, you must win the brain. To do so, you must employ a specific process, speed, and emotional context. If you fail to present information the way your prospects' brains are wired to receive it, it will result in a much more difficult sale where both buyer and seller experience friction and frustration.

The Process

To reach decision-makers early on, you need to gain their attention with insights. These are factual, provocative statements that help frame a prospect's understanding of a reality they are facing. Insights are not meant to close a sale, simply to capture the initial interest required to set your first appointment.

These insights are best when they help prospects understand something about their business they did not before. You're going to have to create some of your own insights and thinking about how you can help them see the world in a different way. Another good way to get started is to ask yourself if there are problems they are unaware of.

Once you have gained their attention, you must find and share a common belief. Your elevator pitch should lead with a belief statement designed to align with your prospect's. This establishes trust early on. It positions you as someone who not only understands them but also as someone who can offer them value.

Once you have established a shared belief, it is time to acknowledge a threat that they are facing. The second part of your elevator pitch accomplishes this. We must acknowledge these threats because it is the surest way to wake up the primitive brain and gain its attention.

Finally, we must position our solution as the way to eliminate the threat. This creates an emotional lift that will awaken the rational part of the brain, working to understand your solution. Now, you are on your way to establishing priority.

Think of it like this chart. We start out at stasis, a neutral state where we are neither presenting a threat nor providing emotional lift. This is when you first walk into the room and align your beliefs. When we set the pain, we force our brains into a threatened state. This is a good thing as it focuses the primitive brain on what you are presenting to it. What we're really after is an emotional lift, but we can't achieve it without establishing the threat that this pain represents. This drives the primitive brain into further action—it is no longer just focused; it is now actively addressing what you are presenting.

WHAT ACTUALLY NEEDS TO HAPPEN

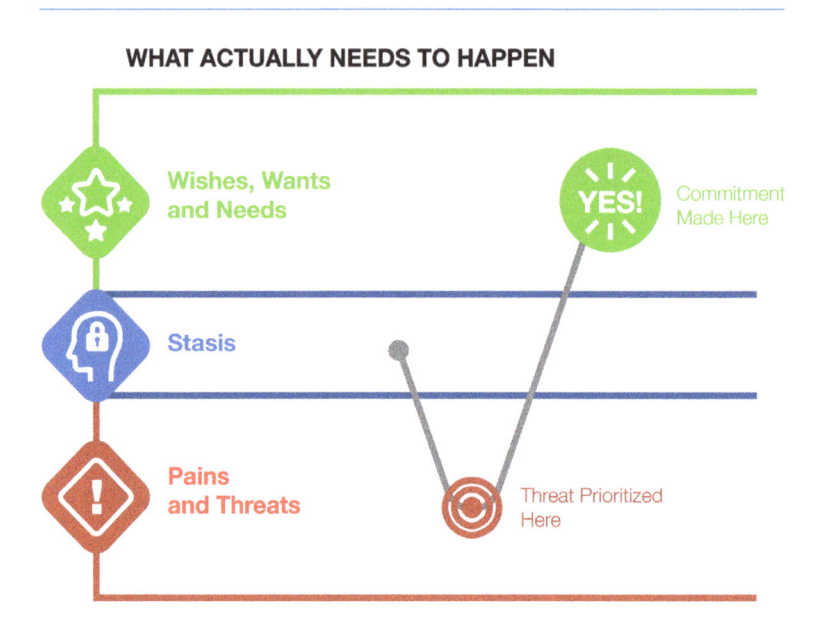

- Wishes, Wants and Needs
- Stasis
- Pains and Threats

YES! Commitment Made Here

Threat Prioritized Here

Now, if we left our prospects down in this valley, we would be bad salespeople. Heck, we would be bad people. The point of driving these threats home is to give them the emotional lift they deserve. Positioning your solution as the way to eliminate that threat is how we will enter the rational brain and establish priority together.

This is absolutely critical.

Think about your prospect. They see things to buy all the time. They are presented with improvements they can make on a daily, weekly, and monthly basis, including yours. There are simply too many ideas to act on them all. The vast majority will never make it past an initial thought. Some get meetings, even interesting ones. Practically none of them become sales.

We know that today only the top priorities get acted on. Top priorities are not necessarily the most logical ideas. They are the ones the primitive brain wants. And they aren't temporary wishes, they're long-term wants. Attention is fleeting, but priority is persistent. Unfortunately, your prospect has a lot of ways to get distracted.

Your Greatest Competitor: Nothing

As salespeople, we often think about a deal only having two outcomes: either you'll win it or your competitor will. That is not the case. The prospect is bombarded with problems to solve and things they can buy to solve them. You may be competing against something completely different than what you sell because resources are limited.

It's difficult enough selling against your competition and against completely unrelated initiatives. But we haven't even addressed the most common obstacle. The easiest thing for your prospect to do, and their favorite course of action, is doing nothing at all.

Much like a soccer game, a sale has more than two outcomes. There is a win and a loss, for sure, but there is also the dreaded draw: choosing no action.

The primitive brain fights hard to get to stasis but not above it. Doing nothing is easy and comfortable. It is nature. In fact, the average salesperson will lose more sales in their career to no decision than they will to all their competitors combined. That is why it is so important to reach priority early and often. Your prospect needs to maintain focus on the priority they have, the one you are going to help them solve.

We tend to think that a delayed decision is not a loss, but it really is. Doing nothing is one of their options, and if they let you down easy by telling you maybe later, they likely just picked the easiest way to break the news.

No decision is a decision, and the decision that won is Not You At This Time. If you are honest with yourself, any answer that is not a Yes. You. Now. Is a loss.

[Diagram: three levels labeled "Wishes, Wants and Needs" (green), "Stasis" (blue), and "Pains and Threats" (red), with a zigzag line moving between Pains and Threats and YES! markers at the Wishes level.]

Over the course of a presentation, you must visit the pain-threat-relief model several times, every five to ten minutes. You must also use this model throughout a meeting to unite a buying committee around the same threat.

Let's take a look at how it works, and how it doesn't, by checking in with our friends, Stan and Fran.

Stan Takes A Typical Approach

Stan knew he had a big opportunity on his hands. There was a lead in his pipeline that would make it all but certain he would not miss his goal a second consecutive quarter.

Stan set up a meeting with five attendees and worked for a week on his presentation. He gathered all the data he could get from his COO and the internet. His delivery would be chock-full of facts they could not argue with.

On the day of the meeting, Stan started with his best stat: the ROI he could deliver for the prospect. Next, he told them about his company and what they did for their customers. They were a leading provider and Stan wanted the prospect to know it.

After telling them about the company, he showed them the specific solution he had in mind for them. They had requested a feature set, so he showed them how the solution checked off everything they asked for.

Next up was a case study, and he had a good one. Stan had sold to their biggest competitor a few years ago and showed them the stats on what they were able to accomplish together.

> Stan wrapped up by showing them the price of the solution, with a trick up his sleeve. First, he showed them the rack rate, but then offered a 10 percent discount that would expire in two weeks.

Stan is not a bad salesperson, but he did not do his prospects any favors. All those stats and facts and figures did not land because the prospects' primitive brains were not ready to receive them. The ROI he promised was questioned and even doubted because he failed to establish trust via mutual belief before that.

The case study did not demonstrate how the prospect would be free of a threat because he never established any threat at all. Instead, the buying committee just thought about losing to their rival while he talked.

When he showed them their own feature requests, he reinforced the prospect's belief that all the solutions in the marketplace are a commodity. After all, everyone else had shown them that list, too. Everyone had a solution that seemed like it would work.

And those pricing games? They are also working against Stan. They show that the solution is not actually that valuable, and if the prospect tries hard enough, they can extend the false deadline and probably even enlarge that false discount.

Unfortunately, Stan's approach is a common one. When his competitors do the same things, it even leads to a few sales.

Sometimes, that discount is enough to separate him from the pack and win a deal or two.

Unfortunately for Stan, Fran had also scheduled a meeting with the same buying committee the very next day. Her approach was a whole lot different than his.

> **How Fran Wins The Brain**
>
> Fran began her meeting by asking three rhetorical questions to the buying committee: Had they ever wondered why they cannot get the right solution set? What if what they got ended up being more work than it was worth? Did they ever wonder why they could not solve this problem before? The members of the committee leaned in.
>
> Immediately after, without stopping for answers, Fran launched into her elevator pitch, sharing what she believes. It instantly created a trust connection among the committee because they believed the same thing. She set a threat and then stated that she and her solution were here to solve that for them. This entire process, from cold introduction to early trust, happened in ninety seconds.
>
> Over the next twelve minutes, she acknowledged three specific pain points she had uncovered,

> answering each with one of her convincing advantages. Every pain she mentioned led to a threat she stated. Each threat was erased when she showed how she was ready to conquer it with them.
>
> After seventeen minutes, her presentation was over. Fran went around the room, asking each member not what they thought, but what they felt. She knew feelings are emotive and emotion becomes the spark generating action. Each time a member of the committee spoke, they were connecting to each other at the primitive-brain level. She saved the CEO for last, so he could hear what his team thought before speaking.

The feedback was positive and engaging. They spent the next twenty minutes in open and honest dialogue around implementation steps and priorities. Since they trusted Fran, she was now a contributor in the group. In fact, she was able to act as leader and facilitator because she knew the solution she was pitching really well. The room trusted her. Fran led the group through the pitfalls and challenges ahead, showing the group what would come next and how the rest of the deal would get done.

A week later, they signed a contract with her company, but Fran knew she had made the sale in the first ninety seconds.

With every meeting, every presentation, every email, everything is on the line. They are moments of truth. Each moment will either advance the sale or end it. There are no do-overs. Sad to say, most selling teams we encounter today present in the exact opposite way our brain's decision-making process needs. That is why so many sales fail to happen at all. They are not being awarded to you or a competitor, they are being lost to third-party priorities or doing nothing at all.

The Rising And Falling Action Of Your Presentation

Never forget you are playing to the real decider, the primitive brain. Keeping its attention requires you to present your pitch in a series of falling action, setting the pain, and acknowledging the threat. You will follow that with the rising action—the emotional lift—of solving it for them.

The primitive brain wants to go back to sleep once you have provided the emotional lift; you will have to repeat the process to keep it engaged. That is what a good movie does every several minutes—it keeps our attention.

In fact, if you want to gain the brain, it's not a bad idea to think of your pitch like taking the prospects to a night at the movie theater.

What type of movie are you going to present to keep brains engaged? This is no time for a thoughtful film that gets the audience pondering important questions. If you want to win the brain, your presentation needs to be more like an action film.

evoke emotion. That is why screenwriting coach Michael Hauge nicknamed Hollywood "The Emotion Picture Capital of the World." An action film evokes strong feelings by taking the audience on an emotional roller coaster of highs and lows; these are tied to the cadence of rising and falling.

Make your presentation a great action film with rises and falls. This is how you keep engaging the primitive brain.

As a reminder, the primitive part of the brain makes its move first, emotion then sparks action, and logic finally comes in as backup support. When you understand that you cannot avoid it, every human decision, including your selling presentation, begins with an assessment of threats, pains, and fears.

Pro Tips

More must be done during the meeting to get the information and access you desire. Here are several must-dos:

No small talk. The clock is running from the moment you enter the room. No preambles. No first introducing the team. No talking about the weather or something in the news. Engage their minds with the three questions.

Stand rather than sit. Stand to make your presentation. The presenter who stands commands more attention than the one sitting at eye level.

Arrive early. Perhaps you have heard the adage: Early is on time, on time is late, and late is unacceptable. If this is business you want, show your respect by arriving plenty early. This will also allow the presentation team to not be so anxious.

Build trust fast. With brains quickly scanning if you are to be believed, it is crucial to establish trust as quickly as possible in your presentation or the various brains in the room will move on to other distractions. You build trust fast by understanding your whys.

Use agendas. An agenda helps you set direction, but also gives prospects the opportunity to tell you what they're thinking. In a good meeting, an agenda will be two-thirds items that you plan to cover, and one-third items that the prospect wants to cover.

Be brain friendly. Study what neuroscience teaches about presentations. Use brain-friendly images. Use brain-friendly messages. Use words that trigger action. Use words that trigger emotions and feelings. More than 90 percent of communication is nonverbal.

Lead With Rhetorical Questions

In Fran's presentation, she opened with three rhetorical questions. This was done on purpose to wake up the primitive brain and get the room's attention. Surprisingly, it also builds your credibility. Think about someone that asks good questions that help you gain insight. You trust them, right? You can do this, too.

Think of the three main problems you are going to solve for the prospect, then frame them in a way that starts with one of the following:

- Ever wonder why _____ ?
- What if _____ ?
- Imagine if _____ .

This takes practice at first and it may feel awkward the first time you open this way. But it is incredibly effective when executed. When your belief and conviction become the emphasis behind these questions, you won't come across as a cheesy salesperson. You will be someone they can trust, someone who understands what they are dealing with and someone who potentially can help them solve a problem.

Close With A Bang, Not A Whimper

It was one of the twentieth century's greatest poets, T.S. Eliot, who said "This is the way the world ends. Not with a bang, but a whimper." He could have been describing most presentations.

Never end the presentation with, "Are there any questions?" Turning control of the conversation over to the decision-making team is ending with a whimper.

To end with a bang, use what we call the Five-Minute Feedback Loop. Announce you are going to do a Five-Minute Feedback Loop. This engages their brains. Tell them you are going to ask them some questions. Your message is, "Help me help you."

Ask what two or three key points stood out. The group will tell you what is important to them. There is power in having them summarize, not you. Then ask what two or three points created or caused confusion. This is vital feedback. The time to correct confusion is at that moment. In teaching, it is called the teachable moment. In presentations, it is the moment you win the brain.

7

Win The Journey

Today's prospects are entering a marketplace that is a whole lot different than it was even ten years ago. In 2011, Google found that for every single purchase, large or small, the buyer consulted an average of more than ten review sources before they bought. For small purchases such as a box of staples or a bar of soap, it was fewer. For large purchases like a vehicle or an investment account, the number was much higher.[3]

While those studies were focused on consumer patterns, the same behavior has crept over into the B2B space. In fact, Gartner and Forrester project that 80 percent of the B2B purchase process occurs without any human interaction at all.[4]

This is the buyer's playbook today—to leave the salesperson out of the picture if they can, and then get all the contenders to compete on price.

You need a way to counteract it, not compete with it. When prospects enter the marketplace, they are trying to solve a problem. They may arrive at the right solution on their own, but most do not. Having an expert by their side early on can be a big, big help.

Think about it this way: Tomorrow when you go into work there is an email at the top of your inbox. Incredibly, it tells you that several billion dollars have been placed in a bank account and you are the account signee.

Unfortunately, it is not yours to spend freely. Instead, you must go out and buy rockets for a mission to Mars that will launch five years from today. Good luck.

Put in a position like this, what is your first move? Do you go to Google and search for something like "Who sells rockets that go to Mars?" That would be absurd, right?

Chances are, you would attempt to find an expert, even multiple experts, to help guide you through the process. You would need to learn how to compare vendors. You would want to know what to ask and how to understand which points are and are not negotiable. You would probably even need to learn how the process works to purchase such a thing.

What if you received an email five minutes later from a department head at NASA offering you some help? Are you annoyed or relieved?

Prospects do not know much more about what you sell than they do about buying rockets that go to Mars. You are the expert that is going to help them solve their problem.

The Three Phases Of The Buying Journey

Let's get back to the buyer's playbook. If you are going to counteract it, you are going to need to understand it well. It is useful to think of the deal happening in three phases, in a beginning, middle, and end kind of way.

Sometimes, they move through these phases almost entirely on their own. Other times, a salesperson is with them the whole way.

Sometimes, prospects will travel them quickly, in a matter of days or even hours. Other times, the phases take months and the prospect may even move backward more than once.

No matter how they happen, you must be prepared to step in, build trust and help them through. Let's take a closer look at these phases:

1. **Early:** This is when a prospect is trying to identify whether the problem they are attempting to solve is a priority. This will help them decide if pursuing a solution of any kind is worth their time and effort. We call this phase the priority phase.

2. **Middle:** During this phase, the prospect is deciding between competing priorities. Constraints on budgets and time pit one problem against another, and can even divide people within the purchasing department. They are considering competing offers for each priority, which muddies the waters even more. To top it all off, they are trying to understand the purchasing process itself, both internally and externally. It can be a lot to take in, and information overload can wreak havoc. We call this phase the planning phase.

3. **Late:** This is when the prospect has named the solution they prefer and is attempting to find suitable arrangements on scope and price. They often have

multiple proposals from providers on the table and they are making two decisions. One, whether they want to buy something or keep doing what they were doing before. Two (and only if they buy something), which offer they should agree to. We call this phase the procurement phase.

Let's take a closer look at each of these phases to understand how best to win the journey and counteract the buyer's playbook.

Priority — **Planning** — **Procurement**

The Priority Phase

Entering at the priority phase represents your best chance to win the deal. But it is also the hardest place to gain access.

Prospects in this phase are typically unaware they are even on a path to purchase. They may have an emerging recognition that they are dealing with a problem, but many have not realized what that problem is just yet.

Meeting prospects in the priority phase is such a challenge—the prospect does not even know they are buying yet. So why on earth would they reach out to a salesperson?

They won't.

Getting access to the right prospects early on requires you, the salesperson, to expend all the effort. We are going to borrow an old-school sales term for this effort and call it hunting.

In many of today's B2B sales organizations, the idea of hunting has gone by the wayside. For some companies, it is nonexistent. Sales reps sit and wait for leads to materialize, then call on those leads. But that is problematic for salespeople.

When a lead comes up, the prospect is often in the late phase of their purchase, the procurement phase. The rest of those leads are leaving the middle—the planning phase—and headed for procurement. To become a lead, they must have done enough research to name their own solution and eventually find you.

That is not to say all leads are bad or that they should not be called on. They are good, and we will address how to deal with them. But the best way to make a sale, the kind that closes quickly and at the margin you want, is with early access. You must hunt, but not in the way you think.

Most hunting activity today is in the form of cold calling. This applies, whether the medium is phone, email, or social media, etc. The pitch (if you want to call it that) basically amounts to: I sell _____. Want any?

This fails for two reasons. First, a decision-maker never answers the phone. And getting past gatekeepers? That's practically impossible. Lower-level employees do not stick out their necks for a stranger on the phone. It represents too big a risk of upsetting their boss.

The second reason this fails is because the message is completely missing the point. If they already know that they want to buy what you sell, "How lucky you called!" they may say. If this is the case, they are in the procurement phase already, anyway.

Finding someone who needs what you sell in this manner requires perfect luck to find leads. That is not hunting.

Successful hunting requires a good message that gets the attention of high-level decision-makers. To accomplish this, you are going to need some insights.

Insights are provocative and true statements that help reframe the prospect's view of their company or their job. They help the prospect recognize a new problem or understand an old one in a new way. Then, they point the prospect in the right direction to solve it. These insights are the best way to get the attention of the right people you want to talk to, earlier in the process. They will open more and better doors for you.

Think about CRM software. When it entered the marketplace, nobody was sitting at a desk, flipping through a rolodex and wishing for a bunch of data entry work. Instead, sales leaders came to understand that institutional knowledge is valuable, but there were two things preventing them from harnessing it: the losses from disorganized data and high turnover in sales roles. When CRM began taking over the B2B world, it was these insights, not features or differentiators, that captured the initial attention of sales leaders. These insights created a multi-billion-dollar industry out of thin air.

Your insights must speak to the issues that real decision-makers have. In the example above, high turnover is not a problem for sales reps. They will go wherever they can get paid the most. Likewise, for the sales rep, disorganized data was not an issue, because they knew exactly where to find what they needed on their own. Good insights filter out the people that cannot make buying decisions, because they only speak directly to the leaders that can.

Do the work to develop good insights and take them into the marketplace. This is how you will gain the attention of your real buyers and open doors early on. Use your elevator pitch to align beliefs and build trust. Now, you are on a path to purchase that keeps you in it the entire way.

Planning Phase

When you enter the planning phase having been present during the priority phase, your primary job is to help them navigate the sale.

Start by gaining an understanding of who will be involved. What are their competing priorities and what objections will they present? You will need a plan to unite the committee, and that plan must involve a shared belief that can align them all.

Think about group alignment like a flag. You are going to run it up the flagpole and point to it whenever the committee goes astray. "Remember this?" you will ask. "That's what we're doing here. Let's not lose sight of it."

During this phase, your job is to keep them focused and help them scope the solution. Align first, then help them navigate, then define the solution.

But what if you are brought in during this stage and weren't around to help them build the priority? There are still wins to be had, but you will have to work hard to stand out from the crowd.

To do this, you will need to be diagnostic at first, and then highly prescriptive. Help them assess the issue with tools and consulting. They might already know the problem. They also might have misdiagnosed or only partially diagnosed the real causes. This will either reinforce the priority—one you can now align with, or change it altogether which is the best outcome when you're brought in at this phase because you have successfully helped them redefine the problem. Now you are the only one who is aligned to their new priority.

From there, relentlessly align your solution to their priority. This will be the separation you need to become the front-runner.

Procurement Phase

When you have been with the prospect from the priority phase on, the procurement phase becomes a nonevent. You have built trust, you have defined the solution together, and it is time to get to work. Job well done.

you enter during this phase, you have your work cut out for you. Unfortunately, most salespeople today enter at this phase. That is when they get the three ugly questions that make it tough to find or align with priority:

Can you do it? Do you want it? How much?

Most leads are in the procurement phase. Any RFP that you did not help write is in the procurement phase. Winning real deals here is exceedingly difficult. And by real, we mean at the margin you wanted on the timeline you wanted. They are tricky, but they can be worth working on.

Priority Planning Procurement

You need to first accept that the salesperson in these situations has little to no influence at this stage. Often, you are being asked to show up and sell on price, not value. You truly have little time for anything else, frankly, because the deal is happening without you.

You can consider one of three strategies to compete for these late-stage deals:

1. Position your sale as the true low-cost solution. This is dangerous because while it may win the deal today, you are subject to ever-lower offers from competitors in the future that will take away your business. This usually only works in the few industries in which repeat business is a nonfactor.

2. Cut out your margins to compete on price, hoping for greater future engagement. This is dangerous because you often won't be able to charge more for the same scope in the future, so this strategy usually only works when you have an additional, different product or service sale that you're confident you can make.

3. Attempt to reconfigure the scope entirely by showing them something they missed in the planning stage. When successful, this helps you unlock new priorities that you can position your solution toward. When unsuccessful, the prospect decides to abandon the priority altogether.

Your Playbook:
1. Get in early by hunting.
2. Find their priority and align with it.
3. Help them navigate the sale, rallying the committee around the flag.
4. Define the scope together.

THE PRIORITY SALE

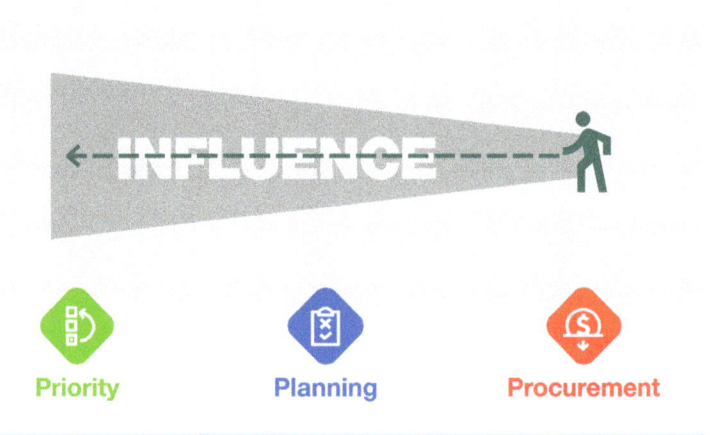

Priority — **Planning** — **Procurement**

5. Close the deal.

8

Win The Deal

Here's a funny story about one of the best meeting outcomes we have ever heard:

We were working with a financial services company on a presentation for a big account. If they won it, it would immediately be their largest client. Right after the meeting, Phil, the lead, called to tell us how it went.

"We only used half our slides," he began, somewhat ominously. "We had the title slide up, and we went around the room to introduce ourselves.

"I got through the first two questions; things seemed to be going well. But then I asked the third question, 'Why does it always feel like you have to do all the heavy lifting when it's supposed to be a partnership?'

"I saw the CEO and the CFO look at each other with wide eyes and open mouths. Then the CEO gave the table in front of him a swift, loud, open-palm slap."

Thwap!

"Phil," he said, dead serious. "That's exactly what we've just been talking about."

"While I delivered our elevator pitch, the CEO kept nodding and saying 'yes.' We spent the next hour and a half having a great conversation." Phil reported. "We almost forgot to show the numbers at the end."

Phil's company won the account.

Winning The Deal Is About Connecting With Their Priority

As we have discussed, winning the deal is all about connecting with, and helping them act on, their priority. On that day, there were probably cheaper bids than Phil's, maybe even better products than his, too. But Phil and his team left the room with something way more important than the lowest price. They had allies, willing to fight for their bid, behind closed doors. That is what it takes today to unite a buying committee.

The procurement phase is, obviously, your last chance to connect with priorities. What is less obvious is how all your prior interactions—each moment of truth leading up to closing—has prepared you to do so.

When you earn entry during the priority phase, you can explore and form priorities alongside your prospect.

This can often be mistaken for relationship building, especially in B2B sales. But relationships do not lead to income. How many times a year do you drop checks in the mail to your friends just to thank them for your relationship?

The bond you need to focus on forming is around a shared belief and priority. This is stronger than bonds formed by common interests outside of work or a shared social connection. You are aligning the reasons why you are doing something together.

That is powerful, but it can only be done when the buyer and seller start the very beginning of the journey together.

Your job, as a seller, is to seek out prospects who likely have a latent priority, something they are not addressing. Help them find it, help them solve it, and you are on the right track to winning the deal.

This is the problem with most leads; when prospects come to you, they have already formed a priority. They think they know the problem they need to solve. That is when they go searching for something and find your marketing materials, along with your competitors'.

Why Digital Marketing Fails So Many B2B Companies

An interesting aside: Digital marketing compounds this problem. Websites are optimized to be found on search engines for the highest-volume keyword phrases. In other words, marketers have been trained to call themselves the same things, because they want the website traffic that comes with it. This leads to some of the commoditization in the marketplace.

Likewise, most digital advertising comes with targeting tools that help narrow the audience that finds you. So, at this point you and your competition are outbidding each other to say the same things to the same people.

This is not to say that traffic isn't valuable or that you should abandon the strategy. Just note that these leads are often from prospects who have already commoditized you with their search phrases.

Problems arise when the salesperson treats these prospects as if they are freshly entering the sale with open hearts, open minds, and open brains. They are not. They have been searching for days, weeks, or even months, and the one doing the searching is most often tasked with procuring a named solution. They have been delegated the task from the real decision-maker who decided ages ago what their own priority was.

With this type of marketing alone, sales is, at its core, request fulfillment. Sure, there are deals to be done here, but they are not the ones that will lead to high margins and happy buyers. They don't require highly trained (or highly paid) sales reps to usher them through the last 20 percent of the sale. The prospect is just going to decide on price, anyway.

This is not a knock on B2B marketers. We have met many and observed that most know how to market to already-established priorities. The problem with this type of traditional marketing is that it merely feeds into the buyer's playbook. For the most part, B2B marketing ends up being nothing more than sales support and fulfillment. Day to day, that means a lot more PowerPoint slide creation, a lot less priority creation.

Knowing these outcomes, it's no surprise that most B2B marketing materials focus on what the company does. A little of it tells how the company does it. Nearly none of it tells a prospect why they should think of a new priority and then drops them off on their sales teams' doorsteps.

So, what do you do about the leads you do get? Certainly, you do not ignore them. They can still turn into valuable deals. These are more difficult sales, though, because you have less time to connect with their priority.

In situations where you have entered the sale in the planning or procurement phases, you might need to fight your instincts; most salespeople want to play it safe, pitch benefits, and not rock the boat. But this prevents you from doing your real job: eliminating pains and threats for your prospect.

Instead, being brought into the very end of the buyer's journey is the time when you have to work the hardest to cause a disruption, to separate yourself as the only solution that will solve the real problem. This is difficult to do. Like the old sayings go: The train has left the station. The horse is out of the barn. Your job is to drag them back into their buying process, to really consider why they are doing this.

They do not want to ask those questions. They are in the phase of asking what instead. We call this kind of sale the three ugly questions, because everything the prospect wants to know boils down to: Can you do it? Do you want it? How much?

This being the case, your job is to think of ways to get the prospect to say, "We hadn't thought of that." That indicates you are on the right track to finding a hidden priority they missed during planning or procurement. Once found, you have the leverage you need to position your solution. It must be compelling enough to overcome the concern of going back and reevaluating.

A few useful ways of doing this can be by asking simple questions. Consider:

> *I'm sure you've seen a lot of proposals, and you know what direction you're headed in. I'm curious to know, what one or two things were you expecting that nobody has included yet?*

Here, the prospect is forced back into the planning phase—possibly even the priority phase—mindset, to ensure that they are really solving the right problem.

Diagnostic tools may also help. When a diagnosis indicates that the root causes are not what is being addressed, you may be able to reform priority around an alternative that does. To execute all of this, you are going to need three things: a desire to improve, relentless honesty, and effective training.

Your Desire To Improve

Most salespeople do not buy and read books on how to improve their sales ability. That you have made it most of the way through one yourself, says a lot about you.

Either you are someone that has a burning desire to improve, or you were given this as an assignment. If it is the latter, this section is for you.

Everyone says they want to get better. But those who achieve greater do something simple, hard, and powerful. They set goals. You can do it too. In a study of nearly two million salespeople, it was found that the reps best at goal setting, those that tested in the top 10 percent, sold more than their peers. A lot more. Three times more.

Goals are easy to dismiss because they are so simple to set, yet are very difficult to achieve. This is where individual performance stalls and sales cultures become nonexistent. When you are not driving toward something—what and by when?—any route, timeline, and approach will do. This is not good and is the reason salespeople do not reach much beyond mediocrity; they do not even know where they are going.

An important distinction, here: the goals that make salespeople successful are not quotas or sales goals given to them by their organizations. Every single B2B sales rep has those. We're talking about individuals who understand why they are in a sales role. Individuals who are working toward something bigger than the numbers they are handed to fulfill each quarter. Here is a formula for setting your own goals to create a roadmap to improvement.

First, start with a vision. This is somewhere you want to be in life in the future. It could be a new car, a vacation home, an education for your children, or anything else that will require a different level of effort or income to achieve. While goals do not necessarily require a vision, they are way more effective with one than without.

Next, figure out what it will take to fulfill that vision. Typically, there are income goals attached to it. Figure out what those are and when you need to achieve them. Let's take the vacation house as an example. You would need to set an income goal to acquire the cash for the purchase or down payment. There are also a few tasks not related to income like finding a place you enjoy and picking out the house.

Then, for each of the tasks it will take to achieve your goal, write down the reasons why—usually about ten reasons—this goal will fail. Write down the date you want to achieve the goal.

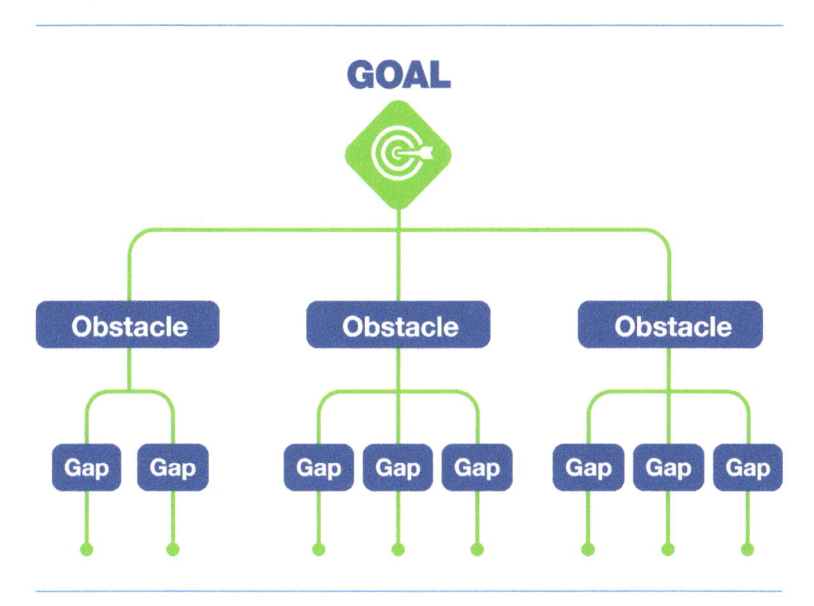

GOAL

- Obstacle
  - Gap
  - Gap
- Obstacle
  - Gap
  - Gap
  - Gap
- Obstacle
  - Gap
  - Gap
  - Gap

That list of reasons why your goal might fail are today's obstacles. Plan for overcoming each of them and track your progress. Maybe you need weekly hunting tasks to fill the pipeline, or perhaps there is a project that will ease the journey ahead. Plan them out and hold yourself accountable.

By the way, that list of reasons you might fail become excuses on the date you wrote next to them. Conquer them while they are obstacles and you will do well to achieve your goals.

A desire to improve is the basis for improvement. We all want more but need the right framework to get there. With it in place, you will find yourself more motivated because the tasks do not seem so impossible to accomplish.

Relentless Honesty

Recall the three phases of the sale from the buyer's perspective: priority, planning and procurement. Prospects can work with salespeople at any of the three. If you leave it up to them, they will first choose to talk to you during the procurement phase. By the time they are ready, it is way too late, every single time.

To start reliably winning more business, you must be honest with yourself about where you are entering the sale. This honesty is required for two reasons.

First, the amount of time available to connect with their priority at each phase is drastically different. So much so that it changes your tactics. At the end of the sale, you're practically out of time before you even start; more drastic interventions may be necessary. They are less effective but better than allowing the primitive brain to shut you out completely. Assessing where each prospect is when you enter the picture will make you more effective at closing deals from the planning and procurement phases.

More importantly, taking an honest look at where you enter your deals should be the first step in motivating action to get in sooner, using better hunting, and aligning techniques. If you are like the vast majority of B2B salespeople, you recognize that almost all your deals are meeting you in the procurement phase. A few are in the planning phase. How many have you met before they were really in the market to buy from you? It is likely very few.

This honesty is needed at both an individual level and an organizational one. Companies need to empower a better selling playbook, and individuals must embrace their role in hunting for higher access, earlier on.

Effective Reinforcement

Think about a successful Broadway show. Every night, and some days, tourists and locals pack theaters in New York City and elsewhere, paying hundreds or even thousands of dollars to be entertained by musicals and plays. The hit *Hamilton* grossed a billion dollars in just a few years.

To achieve that success, it requires a team of professionals executing their own script, every day and night. The relentless attention to details between the set, costume, music, and lyrics is what captivates audiences. What if a Broadway show was run like a typical sales team?

The director and writer (the sales manager and the CEO) would have spent half a year tossing ideas back and forth, getting excited about what they had in store for the cast (the sales staff). They would get the actors together in a room, flying them in from all corners of the country, but forget the orchestra. And for an entire day, they would lay out their vision, showing them what they had in mind. There would be a thirty-minute breakout session for each cast member to practice their part. On day two, they would be put on stage and told to perform it live, in front of a packed house.

Maybe you are more familiar with sports: If a team were run like most sales staffs, training camp would be one day long.

ches would go through each play once and send them in the first game, never practicing again.

The point is that professionals know improvement requires practice. Yet it scarcely exists in sales roles. The annual sales training some companies offer is a good start. So is this book. But neither of them can take the place of continuous training. We need to practice the plays in our own playbook if we ever expect to counteract a buyer's.

This training must come in two ways. First, just like the Broadway cast must practice their parts hundreds of times before performing, salespeople must train themselves on how to find and align to priority. This means continuous reinforcement of the principles along with scenario planning. Humans tend to forget nearly everything they learn after seven days. If you want to get better, you have to commit to continuous reinforcement.

Second, just like an athlete watches films of their own practice and game performances, salespeople must be able to get real feedback from their own actual calls.

New advancements in technology have made it possible for salespeople to see their own performances and improve. Simply recording a Zoom call is a good start. Other tools that AI offers give basic statistics like how much you or your prospect is engaged on the call, or how fast you are talking.

Many initially bristle at the thought of recording themselves or allowing management to. How far you or your organization take these concepts is up to you. For the motivated sales rep, this live feedback is invaluable and welcomed. For motivated organizations that have hungry teams ready to improve, this is a must. Would you be excited to be selling against a competitor doing both of those things?

The Winning Mentality

When Stan gets a lead from his marketing team, everyone celebrates. But when Fran has been working with the CEO of that business for months, helping them find their priority and align her solution to it, Stan never had a chance at all. It was a huge waste of his time.

Deals are won by individuals who are motivated to improve and set goals the right way. They are honest with themselves about where they enter their deals and what they need to do to win once they get there. They earn early access. They work for companies that provide consistent training and feedback tools to help them practice their trade like the professionals they are.

In an accelerating world and given the time it takes to make these things happen, it may seem like an impossible task, but it does not have to be. With the right desire, good goals, and a good partner to help you, these things can be in place in just a few weeks.

9

The New Playbook

So far, we have talked about how important it is to find and align to your prospect's priorities. We have also talked about a lot of tools you need to get there.

Below is what you need to do so you can start executing The Priority Sale. This list is built in the order of how a typical B2B sales organization should execute them. Certain items build on the work of others. The order in which you will deploy these tools is not necessarily the order in which you will create them.

1. Define Your Real Impact

Start your work by finding your real impact, the threats you solve for your prospects. Use the Name That Threat exercise to work through a few iterations of finding their threats and how you can relieve them.

This will be the basis of the rest of the work to follow. Use the question "So what?" several times to ensure you are getting to the root of the problems they are dealing with.

2. Craft Your Elevator Pitch

Every one of your sales will start with your elevator pitch, no matter where you enter. It is your first—and best—chance to begin aligning beliefs, building trust, and gaining priority.

Your elevator pitch must state a belief, set the pain, acknowledge the threat, and position your solution as the relief to that threat. It answers why, not what.

A well-crafted elevator pitch is the answer to the two questions your prospect must answer: Why should we do anything right now? and Why should we choose you?

It is effective because it pitches the way our brains are hardwired to work, starting with the primitive brain and working up to the rational. You will be using your elevator pitch in every initial moment of truth you have with any member of the buying committee.

3. Build Your Convincing Advantages

Your Convincing Advantages are the three ways you will provide relief from their threat. They are an important framework for your conversations, a way to connect your real impact with your prospect's top priorities.

To find your convincing advantages, we'll create two lists. For list A, document all the things your prospect values in a provider like you. This list typically contains between one and two dozen items.

Now group these items together into like categories. For example, if you have fast response times and provide easy resolutions to common problems, these could be considered together in a category great customer service. Once combined, this list will usually be three to seven categories.

For List B, document the top categories that your prospects use to make a buying decision. These are based on the pains and threats they want to solve for themselves so you will have a list of your prospects' threats. Choose the three largest threats.

Align three categories from List A with the three big threats in List B. What you have is a response that your company provides to the threats driving decision-making. We're almost there.

Next, find one or two words that embody that offer assurance. They should demonstrate how you are going to eliminate their threat. For example, if being caught with surprise expenses is a fear your prospects have, you could say that you are transparent or proactive or that you offer accurate budgets.

You will need a separate response for all three threat responses. These should be an alignment of the List A and List B.

Finally, put these three responses together. To make them more memorable, see if you can create some repetition with a common lead-in word. Another great way to make them more memorable is to use alliteration, a common sound in each word (all beginning with an "s" sound, for example.) Bonus points for those that can employ the ultimate memory tool: rhyming.

With your Convincing Advantages in place, you are armed with a tool that can help you answer why and how on the spot, every time. Even better, the companies that have these in place create a common messaging platform for all their salespeople. This is the ultimate brand consistency, rooted in your promise to perform, and delivered by every rep, every time.

Best yet, both companies understand what's being offered and delivered from the very beginning. It is an understanding, not between individuals, but between organizations. In other words, it insulates future business from the relationship sale. If a buyer or seller moves on, the relationship can endure on these terms.

4. Create A Presentation Of Your Convincing Advantages

Your presentation will most often take the form of slide software (PowerPoint and the like) but this is not always the case. Here, we mean presentation to help your prospect understand what you are selling using the convincing advantage framework. This may be with a web page on a Zoom call or a brochure on a conference floor. It could even be the right talk track for a chat in an airport terminal. It could be more than one of these, or all of them, in time.

You want to achieve consistency with this presentation. Every salesperson in the organization must understand the convincing advantage framework and be able to pitch from it, using whatever tool makes the most sense for the team. This should be built in a way that connects with the primitive brain. Map it, using the dips technique.

For each advantage, understand the specific pains and threats it addresses. Your talk track should acknowledge these first. You will then need to provide emotional lift with the specific details of how your solution alleviates those threats. When we map presentations to the emotion of the recipient, these end up looking like a heartbeat pattern, with multiple dips (as we set the pain) and lifts (as we provide the solution).

Map out your presentation according to the emotional pattern of your prospect and make sure everyone understands how to deliver it.

Pro Tip: If you are using a medium—like PowerPoint, a web page, or a brochure—to pitch, it must be highly visual. For humans, vision is the only sense directly wired into the primitive brain. What we see takes priority over what we hear or touch or smell or taste. Know your talk track down pat, but do not put the words on the screen; shoot for showing fewer than seven words. Use visual cues like good photography and thoughtful illustrations to make your points. These are worth spending a few dollars on if you're not artistically inclined.

Keep in mind that your media should accompany your pitch, not be your pitch. In other words, have assets that facilitate a conversation. Don't show up and read from a screen. If necessary, create separate leave-behinds that have more text.

You will travel the planning and procurement phases of your buyer's journey with this presentation. It aligns to priority, helps navigate the sale, and drives the right kind of conversation to mutually define the solution.

5. Find Your Insights

Once you understand your elevator pitch and have a presentation capable of traveling the later stages of the sale, it is time to start building the assets you need to find real decision-makers earlier on. This starts with insights.

Insights are tools you will use to gain the attention of higher-level decision-makers. They are factual, provocative statements that help frame a prospect's understanding of a reality they are facing. They help clarify, explain, or present problems in previously unknown ways.

For our company, RPG, the three deadly Cs are an insight. They help sales leaders understand and name specific threats that they always felt but never put into words. Framing their reality in this way provides clarity, a problem to solve.

Creating insights is a challenge and many organizations that set out to accomplish it get mired in the weeds before they can find what they are looking for. Here is a process that can work:

Think about who you sell to most often. Are they the real decision-makers? Go up the organizational chart one level. What would it look like if you sold to them instead? We are going to keep that person in mind as we move on.

Now think about their day-to-day pains. What do they deal with that they would rather not? These do not even have to be things that you can solve for them. Do not limit yourself; put them all on the board.

Now, we are going to ask three questions to try to arrive at our insights. Keep in mind that, at this point, we do not need the answers to be known to be true. We will get to that. These answers can be simply ways that we feel to be true.

    a) What does your organization know that could help them with this pain or threat, right now? If you got their attention and could have an honest conversation with them, what would you tell them? In other words, what do you wish they knew?

b) What does your industry, your competitors or even (gulp) your company do that makes it worse? Be honest. Why does that happen? What could your prospect understand about these things that would prevent or fix them?

c) What could your organization do to alleviate this pain or threat that you do not do today? Could it be easily implemented? Would it be worth it?

The answers are the basis of your insights.

For the final step, it is important to find some proof points for your answers. The proof is not for leading in with because the primitive brain is your gatekeeper, but you will need to pass the test of the rational brain to get it to rubber-stamp what the primitive brain encountered.

Your proof points can often come from your own data. How many times have you worked on a project that had an issue like X and an outcome like Y? It is OK to be imprecise but do not be disingenuous; tell people things like "in our experience" and "about this amount of the time," but do not make things up.

Outside data sources may also be available to you with a bit of research. This research may be the kind that requires more than a search engine, and there could be outside sources of data or other industry experts you can talk to that will help.

6. Hunt For Higher Priority

Your insights are valuable tools to gain attention, but they will not sell on their own. You need a good campaign to get in front of real decision-makers, and your insights are just the leading edge. Fundamentally, this campaign needs two parts—the attention-gaining outreach and the follow-up presentation needed to start framing and forming priority.

Your outreach campaign may consist of any or a combination of webinars, emails, phone calls, advertising, content marketing, and more. You know your industry and should choose your medium based on what you think will work best. If you have marketing expertise in the organization, leverage it to build these items.

Lead with your insights and do not be afraid to tease the answer. In some cases, it will be worth booking the appointment to get it. In most cases, it is fine to deliver the entire insight and ask if they would take the time to talk about some ways to use this new information for their own benefit. Remember, you are the helpful expert that is going to help them solve a real problem.

When prospects buy from sellers this way, they appreciate the sale and the thing they purchased more. When they enter the marketplace on their own, they leave that helpful expertise out until the very end and never actually engage it. That can lead to frustration and buyer's remorse. Without an expert, they often end up with an incomplete or entirely wrong solution; it lacks the alignment to organizational priority so it's never really appreciated.

To hunt effectively, you will need to:

- Use your insights to gain appointments.
- Use your time together to build priority.
- Start your initial presentation, the first time you are invited, with your elevator pitch.
- Build a presentation that focuses on your insights and what to do about them.
  - Then, close with your convincing advantages and how your solution delivers on your insight.
  - Use the dips model to map the emotional response and put together that content before reaching out.
- Effectively find your prospect's real threats by establishing trust and posing thoughtful questions.

7. Enable Yourself And Your Organization

Here's a funny thing about sales roles today—most of the formal education on the subject lies in the business sector, outside academia. Despite the abundance of sales positions in the United States today, most salespeople are given little to no formal education in sales. This is one reason why sales organizations continually fail in this area. Potentially worse, the ones that do engage have an outdated view of what training is or how it should work. Many sales leaders lament that training is not held accountable for results. But because they're relying on methods from the '60s to get it right, it was bound to fail from the very beginning.

Modern training must resemble the relentless commitm of the Broadway cast or the professional sports team. Practice must be continuous if results are to be expected, and the material being taught has to have been invented since email and the search engine (let alone the cell phone and the fax machine).

Today's sales training should be a combination of lessons that sales staff can complete at their own pace and are crucial because they can be referenced over and over, reinforcing the concepts they teach. The lessons must be accompanied by instructor-led training, whether virtual or in person. Training sessions, most effective once modules have been completed, close the feedback loop and help staff understand concepts in new ways that lesson modules cannot.

Today's Winning Teams

- Shed antiquated ideas of branding in favor of positioning themselves directly alongside their prospects' top priorities

- Use insights to get in earlier and build trust

- Close big deals from behind a screen because they can drive priority, which is different and more powerful than a relationship

- Deliver pitches that connect to the primitive brain to drive priority

- Put the right players in the right positions using objective data
- Record and replay their own sales interactions to drive personal growth
- Train relentlessly to improve how they hunt, align, navigate, and define the sale
- Use CRM as a sales enablement tool, not a rearview mirror

Putting It Together

None of these to-dos are easy, but they can be done quickly with a dedicated leadership team committed to stay relevant in a rapidly accelerating world. When executed the right way and done together, they can transform sales organizations.

10

Into The Future

Let's recap the hard truths about The Priority Sale and then look into the crystal ball for what is ahead.

Ask any CEO what causes them to sweat on any given day. More than likely, they are experiencing a great level of anxiety about simply keeping up—let alone excelling—in a rapidly changing world.

In *Thank You for Being Late: An Optimist's Guide to Thriving in the Age of Accelerations*, Thomas Friedman notes the rate of change is coming from all directions—technology, the environment, and the marketplace. Without evolving, companies are at risk of becoming irrelevant. Within a matter of months, they can face the prospect of being digitally dislocated if their environments are being altered so quickly that everyone starts to feel they cannot keep up.[5]

This is unsettling. While CEOs always have had to ensure their institutions were evolving more quickly and strategically than their competitors, that pressure has reached an entirely different level. No one is immune. The ability to adapt quickly has become a matter of survival for companies of all sizes and industries.

The Reign Of The "Sales Guy"

Shifts break things. Some are big and others are so big they change the very fabric of our world. Everybody knows technology has profoundly impacted the way we do business and the way we live. While most organizations have found ways to evolve their marketing efforts by investing heavily in tactics like digital marketing and CRMs, few have stopped to ask, "How does our sales team even fit into today's buyers' journey?" What is their function, and how can they win in the modern world?

This shift from the Sales Guy Era to the Age of Acceleration has created three deadly Cs to revenue growth that are plaguing your teams. Commoditization, compressed selling time and consensus decision-making all require a complete overhaul to how you differentiate, present, and close on business. Those who actively attack these changes will create outsized gains; those who stay passive will perish. Consider yourself forewarned.

The first signs of the shift may have seemed trivial by today's standards since they did not cause much pain or loss. They looked like the buyer who had printed out some of your competitors' web pages, or the first time a committee of sudden experts took control of your presentation to grill you with in-depth questions.

Once the losses started stacking up, you might have realized there was something going on. What you didn't know is that your prospects had gradually been cutting you out of large parts of the sales process, making short lists on their own and using information that they found on their own, without you.

Top Five Challenges Facing Sales Organizations
1. It has become harder to stand out, and you are frustrated by continually being cast as no different than your competitors.

2. You can't get the right meetings with the right people at the right times.

3. Your sales team is losing too many close deals, ones they should have nailed.

4. Delayed decision-making is more common than ever.

5. Your team keeps attempting to offer or is being asked for price concessions.

The research, information gathering, and short listing in the early part of a sale used to require a sales rep. Now, it is done online and the place where your crew used to shine does not exist anymore. You lost your access, and in turn, have lost your time to influence and build relationships. Your charm does not get you through the early stages of a sale anymore.

Before the shift, you contacted your prospects while they were forming short lists. You were the gatekeeper of most—or even all—of the information about your products and services that your prospects collected and considered. An added bonus in being early: Your prospects had to put in a lot more effort to bring in one of your competitors. It was much easier to win without them looking around at others, and far be it for you to suggest they do so.

Now, with easy-to-access content and education without direct salesperson involvement, guess where we have evolved? It is too easy for your prospect to bring in as many as a dozen options and put them all on the table in front of you.

Before, you could communicate the reasons why you should make their short list and convince them to let you pitch. Today, you get precious few moments of truth to convince them, all of them, in one interaction.

By no means does this imply your sales team is less important or has less impact on revenue growth. What it does mean is their role has changed in a big way. They must accomplish so much more in a fraction of the time than they used to. This shift has given birth to the three deadly Cs that have redefined today's selling landscape.

You Need Tools To Climb Today's Steep Slope

If your pitch did not immediately hit the mark and make a major impact, you have just dropped way down to the bottom of the prospect's list. Why? Once you have entered the ring, they are typically already extremely far down the buying path, 80 percent of the way along, according to the research of Revenue Path Group. This steep slope can mean fast failure, with no room for error when working to gain additional access.

Worse news: Even if your rivals do not stand out, you are still not getting called back. Your prospects just lose interest and move on to some other pain to solve. Since no one was able to demonstrate that the relief was greater than the cost, the prospect is willing to continue dealing with the pain.

No decision? No big deal to your prospect, but no deal at all for you. It's why so many leads are lost to doing nothing at all with the prospect deciding to not buy anything.

You Need Tools To Overcome Sameness

Today, your prospect has complete access to all your direct competitors at their fingertips. Everyone is just a click away. To your prospect, they all look and sound just like you and it is hard to tell the difference between you and another choice.

This is bad for your prospects; they deserve to know the real differences so they can make better buying choices, and it is bad for your revenue; when all options seem the same, price becomes too much of a deciding factor.

When you cannot clearly differentiate, you are either forced to play games with your pricing or you are more likely to become part of the 60 percent of sales that are lost to no decision at all. Either way, it is wreaking havoc on your margins.

You Need Weapons To Fight Death By Committee

Remember when you could count on one person to help you steer your deal? Not anymore. Decision-making teams are getting bigger all the time. According to Challenger Inc., who continues to do research on the subject, the average size of the committee in 2018 was as large as 10.2 members.[6]

Aligning this huge group around one priority isn't easy, but it's the only way to win today's B2B sale.

What Have We Learned?

Aligning with priorities of real decision-makers is the best way to make a sale. It creates happier buyers, easier closings, and sells you in at higher margins. To accomplish this daunting task, there are three things you must do.

First, you need to understand how your prospect's mind really works. Knowing the process, speed, and emotional context to decision-making, you must create pinpoint messaging that is unique and presented in the way your prospect's brain wants it. This lets you do more in less time because you are perfectly in sync with your prospects, not fighting for their attention. Understanding your prospect's decision-making process allows you to overcome compressed sales times.

Second, you want to learn how to win those close deals, no longer losing what should have been yours all along. You need to quickly lock down their primitive brain with friendly visuals and proofs to drive emotional lift. Giving your prospects the reasons you are different is not enough—they need to understand why action is required now, and why you are the right one to help them. This is the path to overcome commoditization because they finally understand why you are different, better, and fit their priority.

Helping them understand why they must act now is essential to win against other, unrelated priorities they are considering. This cannot be a product of a false deadline; it must be priority-driven, according to threats they already had, not new ones you have created.

Third, you must understand that every single interaction with a prospect every single time is a moment of truth. Each moment is yours to advance or lose the sale. Sales leaders spend a lot of time thinking of how to unify their team, but real pros spend their time unifying the prospect's team. They are getting into deals earlier and rallying prospect teams around their shared priority. They are standing out in the crowded field.

This does not happen on its own or even after a session or two with the whole team. It takes commitment and dedication. You must practice. You must reinforce. You must use tools that can help produce coachable moments.

Finally, You Can Beat The Three Deadly Cs

You can beat commoditization by using messages in line with the order, speed, and emotional context your prospect's brain expects. You can overcome compressed selling time by quickly helping them understand why they should do something now and why they should choose you to help them. You can make consensus easier by aligning your prospects with one great pitch.

Why Other Sales Techniques Are Failing You Now

The three Cs are post-shift obstacles. Other sales techniques and sales training courses do not address them because they were all developed before it.

Compile the top sales training programs for complex sales via any method you like. When we cross-referenced several reputable sources to compile a list of eight, it revealed that all but one of them—seven of the eight most popular—were developed before the internet, personal computers, or cell phones. These well-known, older programs were created when the salesperson influenced 100 percent of the sales journey. They obviously don't today. Something has to give.

Post-shift prospects are vastly different. They are relying on the sales reps to help them make sense of the very final part of the sale, comfort them, show value, and show how they are different—often in one hour or less.

Old Versus Now Versus Next

We are here ↓

OLD	NOW	NEXT
You used to have complete control of the sales process from the start.	Buyers are 70 percent through the journey before you are invited in.	Buyers will cut out the salesperson entirely if they can. They will use AI and other methods to choose between offers.
You were the lead salesperson generating and nurturing interest.	Your website is creating and nurturing leads. You are reduced to the final 30 percent of the sale.	Google and others will create tools to help buyers make sense of the information overload they are experiencing. Great messaging will stand out, but it will not come from salespeople.
You were able to leverage relationship and influence to get that old B&R (bonding and rapport) time in.	You train to pitch and persuade to gain additional insight and access.	Shared priority will be the only relationship that can build enough trust to execute a sale.
You walked one or two buyers through deep discovery and analysis.	You have to pitch a room full of buyers evaluating you.	Buying committees will continue to grow in response to increased budget pressures and organizational priorities.
You trained for a predictable sales journey with few potential options and outcomes.	You have to pitch a room full of buyers evaluating you against competitors, new priorities, and doing nothing at all.	Prospect organizations will create structures for weighing budget priorities against each other, rather than allocating budgets to departments in a use-it-or-lose-it fashion.

This is where The Priority Sale exists—between what is happening now and what is happening next. The individuals, and especially the teams, who adopt this mentality will experience a world in which their buyers are happier. They will find themselves enjoying their position as an early expert to help guide the sale. They will take the stress and anxiety out of selling and turn closing into a nonevent. The future belongs to these individuals.

It will not be easy, but it will be worth it.

APPENDIX

Acknowledgments

Thanks to our colleagues at RPG for contributing to the ideas in this book and for your roles in helping us put The Priority Sale into action every day.

Thank you to our clients, past and present, for allowing us to be a part of your transformations as you work to stay relevant.

Thanks to our publisher, Indie Books International, and especially Henry DeVries, whose expertise and patience is the reason you hold this book in your hands today.

This book is dedicated to the millions of sales professionals working today, especially those who have ever stayed up at night wondering, "Why is this so hard all of a sudden?"

About The Authors

Bryan Gray, Paul Davison, Jesse Laffen, and Mike Rendel are partners at Revenue Path Group (RPG). Every day, they work with sales leaders who are fighting to stay vital and relevant by combatting the three deadly Cs.

Works Referenced

1. Kahneman, Daniel. *Thinking, Fast and Slow* (New York: Farrar, Straus and Giroux, 2013).

2. Sinek, Simon. *Start With Why* (New York: Portfolio, 2011).

3. Mullally, Joan and Andrew P. Simon. *Mastering Google's Zero Moment of Truth in Your Online Marketing* (New York: Eternal Spiral Books, 2011).

4. "CSO Update: The New B2B Buying Journey and Its Implication for Sales," *Gartner*, https://www.gartner.com/en/sales/insights/b2b-buying-journey.

5. Friedman, Thomas. *Thank You for Being Late: An Optimist's Guide to Thriving in the Age of Accelerations* (New York: Picador, 2017).

6. Wixom, Spencer, "84 percent of customers report a buying journey taking longer than expected," *Challenger, Inc.*, November 21, 2018, https://www.challengerinc.com/blog/more-b2b-decision-makers-want-in/.

WANT MORE?

ACTIVATE WHAT YOU'VE LEARNED.

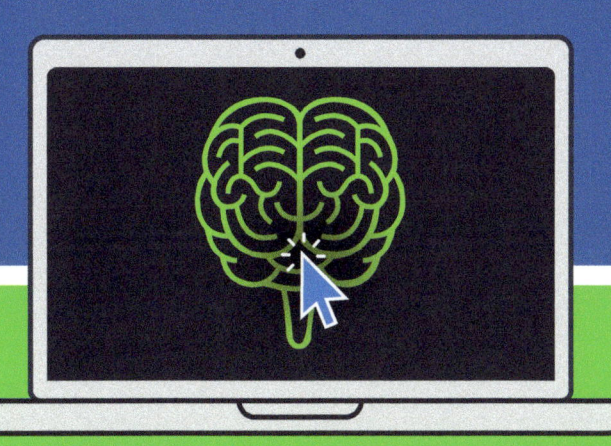

SCAN ME

Learn more about how to implement The Priority Sale as a seller or as a team.

Resources, Training, Newsletter and More!

www.theprioritysale.com

CPSIA information can be obtained
at www.ICGtesting.com
Printed in the USA
LVHW071123230721
693495LV00030B/2253